ADVENTURE LIST

CENTRAL AUCKLAND
- 01 DOMAIN WINTERGARDENS
- 02 LOVERS' WALK
- 03 CORNWALL PARK
- 04 ARCH HILL MTB PARK
- 05 OAKLEY CREEK WATERFALL — 14
- 06 MAUNGAKIEKIE | ONE TREE HILL — 15
- 07 HOBSON BAY EAST PATH — 16
- 08 HUKANUI RESERVE — 17
- 09 KEPA BUSH PATH — 18
- 10 MAUNGAREI | MOUNT WELLINGTON — 19
- 11 MAUNGAREI SPRINGS WETLAND — 20
- 12 MEOLA REEF RESERVE — 22
- 13 MOUNT EDEN PATH — 24
- 14 ŌRĀKEI BASIN PATH — 26
- 15 ACHILLES POINT — 27
- 16 PANMURE BASIN PATH — 29
- 17 TĀHUNA TŌREA NATURE RESERVE — 30
- 18 WAIATARUA RESERVE WETLAND — 33
- 19 WEONA-WESTMERE WALKWAY — 34
- 20 WESTERN SPRINGS PATH — 37

CITY ADVENTURES — 38
- 21 SPLASH PADS — 40
- 22 PUMP TRACKS AND BIKE PARKS — 42
- 23 PLAYGROUNDS — 44

CITY BIKE RIDES — 45
- 24 TĀMAKI DRIVE — 45
- 25 THE LIGHTPATH — 45
- 26 WESTHAVEN BOARDWALK — 45

NORTH AUCKLAND — 46
- 27 CHELSEA ESTATE HERITAGE PARK — 48
- 28 STOKES POINT RESERVE — 49
- 29 LUCAS CREEK WATERFALL — 50
- 30 Ō PERETU | FORT TAKAPUNA — 51
- 31 WAI MANAWA | LE ROYS BUSH — 54
- 32 NORTH HEAD HISTORIC RESERVE — 56
- 33 TAKARUNGA | MOUNT VICTORIA — 59
- 34 WOODHILL FOREST MTB PARK — 61
- 35 RIVERHEAD FOREST MTB PARK — 62
- 36 SANDERS RESERVE — 63

REGIONAL PARKS — 65
- 37 DUDER REGIONAL PARK — 65
- 38 LONG BAY REGIONAL PARK — 65
- 39 SHAKESPEAR REGIONAL PARK — 65

HAURAKI GULF — 66
- 40 RANGITOTO ISLAND — 68
- 41 ROTOROA ISLAND — 72
- 42 KAWAU ISLAND — 76
- 43 TIRITIRI MATANGI ISLAND — 76
- 44 MOTUTAPU ISLAND — 76

EAST AUCKLAND — 80
- 45 TE NAUPATA | MUSICK POINT — 82
- 46 PIGEON MOUNTAIN — 83
- 47 MOTUKARAKA | FLAT ISLAND — 85

- ... WAY — 87
- ... TERFALL — 88
- ... — 89
- ... — 91
- ... — 92
- ... DGE — 94
- 54 TAWHITOKINO BEACH PATH — 96
- 55 WAHARAU BUSH PATH — 98

WEST COAST — 100
- 56 MURIWAI BEACH — 102
- 57 MAUKATIA GANNET PATH — 104
- 58 MITCHELSON LOOKOUT — 106
- 59 MAUKATIA | MĀORI BAY — 107
- 60 TE HENGA | BETHELLS BEACH — 108
- 61 LAKE WAINAMU — 113
- 62 PIHA BEACH — 115
- 63 TE WAHA POINT — 116
- 64 MARAWHARA WALK — 118
- 65 TE PIHA | LION ROCK — 119
- 66 KITEKITE FALLS — 120
- 67 TASMAN LOOKOUT AND THE GAP — 122
- 68 MERCER BAY PATH — 124
- 69 KAREKARE BEACH — 126
- 70 PŌHUTUKAWA GLADE WALK — 128
- 71 KAREKARE FALLS — 131
- 72 WHATIPŪ BEACH — 132
- 73 HUIA POINT LOOKOUT — 133
- 74 WHATIPŪ BEACH SEA CAVES — 135

WAITĀKERE RANGES — 136
- 75 LARGE KAURI WALK — 139
- 76 UPPER NIHOTUPU DAM — 140
- 77 ARATAKI VISITOR CENTRE — 142
- 78 LOOKOUT — 145
- 79 PLANT ID LOOP — 145
- 80 NATURE TRAIL — 145
- 81 LOWER NIHOTUPU DAM — 143

SOUTH AUCKLAND — 146
- 82 AMBURY REGIONAL PARK — 148
- 83 AMBURY FORESHORE PATH — 152
- 84 MĀNGERE MOUNTAIN — 149
- 85 MĀNGERE LAGOON PATH — 151
- 86 WATERCARE COASTAL WALKWAY — 154
- 87 ŌTUATAUA STONEFIELDS — 156
- 88 PUHINUI STREAM FOREST TRAIL — 159
- 89 TŌTARA PARK MTB TRACK — 160

KIWI GUARDIANS' MAPS
- 90 Ō PERETU | FORT TAKAPUNA — 52
- 91 NORTH HEAD HISTORIC RESERVE — 58
- 92 KAWAU ISLAND — 77
- 93 TIRITIRI MATANGI ISLAND — 78
- 94 ŌMANA REGIONAL PARK — 86
- 95 TE HENGA | BETHELLS BEACH — 110
- 96 AMBURY REGIONAL PARK — 150
- 97 AUCKLAND BOTANIC GARDENS — 158

For Finn, my adventuring buddy.

INFORMATION ICONS

Green indicates what is suitable and permitted during the adventure.

Orange indicates that some conditions apply. Please read the activity description for more information.

Red icons indicate what isn't permitted or is unsuitable for the adventure.

PENGUIN

UK | USA | Canada | Ireland | Australia
India | New Zealand | South Africa | China

Penguin is an imprint of the Penguin Random House group of companies, whose addresses can be found at global.penguinrandomhouse.com.

Penguin Random House New Zealand

First published by Outdoor Kid®, 2019
This updated edition published by Penguin Random House New Zealand, 2022

10 9 8 7 6 5 4 3 2 1

Text and photography © Outdoor Kid®, 2022, unless otherwise credited

The moral right of the author has been asserted.

All rights reserved. Without limiting the rights under copyright reserved above, no part of this publication may be reproduced, stored in or introduced into a retrieval system, or transmitted, in any form or by any means (electronic, mechanical, photocopying, recording or otherwise), without the prior written permission of both the copyright owner and the above publisher of this book.

Prepress by Soar Communications Group
Printed and bound in China by RR Donnelley

A catalogue record for this book is available from the National Library of New Zealand.

ISBN 978-1-76104-860-9

penguin.co.nz

MIX
Paper | Supporting responsible forestry
FSC® C144853

Outdoor Kid and the Outdoor Kid logo are registered trademarks.

While care has been taken to write about the adventures in this book, please understand that things can change and the author is not liable for any loss, injury, or inconvenience caused by using this book. For current track information, contact the Department of Conservation. Please take care while having fun outdoors.

Kid-friendly adventures
AUCKLAND
THE ULTIMATE FAMILY GUIDEBOOK

Ceana Priest

HAPPY ADVENTURES!

Auckland is the perfect stomping ground for intrepid explorers who want to clamber up ancient volcanoes, squelch through tidal mudflats and picnic in spooky sea caves. We have loved exploring the region and include our favourite adventures in this guidebook. After Finn was born, I struggled to find trails suitable for buggies and his little legs – memorably ending up knee-deep in a lake on a 'buggy-friendly' trail! So I started Outdoor Kid and began sharing our walks and bike rides. I wanted to help families find adventures that would instil a love of the outdoors into their mini-explorers – and not have to head home after unexpectedly meeting stairs while out with the buggy or bike. Happy adventuring and we hope you'll discover the joys of dune-surfing, lagoon wading and learning about New Zealand's remarkable native flora and fauna along the way.

Ceana and Finn x

Outdoor Kid | Ceana Priest
E. hello@outdoorkid.co.nz
W. outdoorkid.co.nz

BEFORE YOU GO

PLANNING
Make sure your trip suits the abilities of ALL family members. Take a map, or download one to your phone. Share your plans with others, and tell them when you expect to be home.

WEATHER
Always check weather conditions (metservice.com) before heading outdoors on an adventure. Things can change fast.

BE PREPARED
Make sure you have enough food and drink to match the length and conditions of your walk.

TOP TIP
KEEP A SPARE SET OF WARM CLOTHES AND A TOWEL IN THE CAR.

GEAR TO TAKE

BASIC FIRST-AID KIT
For cuts, bruises and bites

INSECT REPELLENT
For pesky biters

RAIN AND WIND JACKET
For all conditions

WATER BOTTLES
Filled up

MOBILE PHONE
Fully-charged

LOTS OF SNACKS
Aka bribes!

SUNGLASSES AND HATS
Summer is hot hot!

EXTRA WARM LAYERS
Just in case

IN AN EMERGENCY CALL 111

WHAT TO WEAR
STAY COOL IN SUMMER AND TOASTY WARM IN WINTER

WARM OUTER LAYER
No matter what the weather conditions are when you start your adventure, always take a warm outer layer like a jumper or a polar fleece top. Even on hot days, it can be much cooler in the forest. So, you may quickly chill when you stop to play beside a stream or for a picnic.

INSIDE YOUR BAG
Slip in a waterproof and windproof jacket just in case. And, it doubles as something to sit on when it's time for lunch. Don't forget to pack plenty of snacks and water too.

HAT AND SUNGLASSES
Protect yourself from the sun's UV rays. Levels are especially high between September and April. Even when it's cold and cloudy, remember to slip, slop, slap and wrap. A thermal beanie when the temperature cools is vital to keep your head warm.

BASE LAYER
For adventures during cold weather, your base layer should fit snugly to your body to trap in body heat. Try and avoid cotton, which takes AGES to dry if it gets wet. Synthetic or merino materials perform much better as a base layer.

In summer, wear something loose-fitting with room for a cool breeze to sneak in.

SHOES
Hiking boots with grippy tread are great if you're exploring in the mountains. Sneakers are perfectly fine for adventures closer to home. Save an old pair, so it doesn't matter if they get muddy.

JUST IN CASE!
What could you spot with a pair of binoculars? Perhaps a native kererū/wood pigeon crash-landing through the trees? Take a photo! Or, grab your pencil and sketchbook and sit quietly in the forest, drawing native plants. Up for an adventure? Grab the torch and go glow-worm hunting.

WHAT TO TAKE

THE GAP, PIHA

OUR TOP SPOTS

OUR FAVOURITE
TOP SPOTS TO EXPLORE

WATERFALLS
Head east for a picnic beside the picturesque 30-metre-high **HŪNUA FALLS** (right, p91).

Need to do some summer toe-dipping? **TE AUAUNGA/ OAKLEY CREEK WATERFALL** (p14) is plonked on Auckland's longest urban stream.

VOLCANOES
Stroll up the iconic **MAUNGAKIEKIE/ONE TREE HILL** (right, p15) and imagine what life was like for nearly 5,000 people in this former Māori pā/fortified village.

A volcano covered with bright red and white mushrooms? Visit **TAKARUNGA/ MOUNT VICTORIA** (p59) and discover why these unusual fungi are popping up everywhere!

BLACK-SAND BEACHES
Fancy some dune-surfing? Visit **TE HENGA/ BETHELLS BEACH** (right, p108) and jump into the lagoon, before clambering up ancient dunes at **LAKE WAINAMU** (p113).

Can you spot the rarest penguin in the world at **MURIWAI BEACH** (p102)? Learn about the kororā/little penguin (p111).

ISLANDS
Visit the largest pōhutukawa forest in the world on **RANGITOTO ISLAND** (p68) and clamber through 600-year-old lava caves.

At low tide, visit Beachlands and walk out to **MOTUKARAKA/FLAT ISLAND** (above, p85), an island tantalisingly perched at the end of a shell bank. Fun muddy tidal adventure!

MANGROVES
Stroll along the meandering **HOBSON BAY EAST PATH** (right, p16) and see if you can spot the unusual tītiko/mudflat snail.

The **TĀHUNA TŌREA NATURE RESERVE** (p30) is a birdwatcher's paradise, so bring your binoculars. And don't miss exploring the exposed sand bar at low tide.

MORE ADVENTURES ONLINE AT:
WWW.OUTDOORKID.CO.NZ

MAUNGAWHAU | MOUNT EDEN

CENTRAL AUCKLAND

EXPLORE THE
CENTRAL CITY

Stroll around an urban bird sanctuary at Western Springs and let the kids loose on the playground. Or, visit Cornwall Park's sprawling farm which surrounds the iconic Maungakiekie/One Tree Hill – visit in spring to see bouncing cute lambs.

HIGHLIGHTS

RAINY DAY? ADMIRE THE PRICKLY CACTUS AND TROPICAL PLANTS AT THE AUCKLAND DOMAIN WINTERGARDENS.

This all-season adventure takes you through two Victorian glasshouses with paths winding through a lush palm forest and past colourful seasonal plants (p10).

COOL OFF BY HAVING A SUMMER PADDLE BY THIS HIDDEN BUSH-CLAD WATERFALL.

Meander alongside the city's longest urban stream, Te Auaunga | Oakley Creek Waterfall, which is surrounded by greenery teeming with native critters (p14).

WALK ACROSS THE TIDAL MUDFLATS AT TĀHUNA TŌREA NATURE RESERVE TO A SANDSPIT AT LOW TIDE.

Here is the perfect adventure for budding birdwatchers. Or, if all things avian are not appealing, then the sandspit turns into an intrepid kid-friendly experience at low tide (p30).

9

CENTRAL AUCKLAND

PARNELL
AUCKLAND DOMAIN WINTERGARDENS

Once a testing ground for exotic fish and plant species in the 1880s, Pukekawa/ Auckland Domain is now an urban oasis with the impressive neo-classical Auckland Museum building lording over the sprawling 75 hectares.

Home to vibrant tropical flowers, prickly cacti and temperate-loving plants, the Wintergardens is an all-season delight with its two Victorian glasshouses.

Cold outside? Loiter in the heated glasshouse with its ferocious-looking cacti and cold-fearing plants. Then, trot past the sunken garden into the cooler glasshouse with its colourful display of hanging plants.

The Domain is Auckland's oldest park and the two barrel-vaulted display glasshouses were built after the grand Auckland Exhibition of 1913–14, held on the same site.

After admiring the plants, walk through the small archway leading to a native fernery. Wind down the path into the former scoria quarry with its small pond – which feels like a fairy grotto.

The duck pond beside the café is fed by an underground spring, and the overflow follows alongside the kid-friendly Lovers' Walk.

Sports fields now cover about 10 hectares of the 50,000-year-old volcanic crater. The surrounding rim creates a natural amphitheatre and is perfect for launching kites.

PUKEKAROA

To the west of the museum, you can still see the small scoria cone Pukekaroa, which means the 'hill of the black-backed gull'.

It is the central scoria cone of the Domain's crater and was the site of a Ngāti Whātua pā.

Carvings surround a sacred tōtara tree to commemorate warrior Pōtatau Te Wherowhero, the first Māori King, who once lived here.

GLASSHOUSE HOURS

In winter, from 1 April to 31 October, the glasshouses are open from 9am to 4.30pm every day.

In summer, from 1 November to 31 March, the glasshouses are open Monday to Saturday from 9am to 5.30pm and on Sunday from 9am to 7.30pm.

Admission is free.

10

CENTRAL AUCKLAND

PARNELL
LOVERS' WALK

This mini-adventure has excellent tree-climbing opportunities and in summer provides a shady retreat from the mid-day sun. Bring a picnic and lie under the trees while watching the kids test out their climbing skills.

This bush-walk is excellent for little legs and has some cool kid-friendly highlights. Look over the curved boardwalk at the trickling waterfall and feel transported to the tropics while standing among the lush towering palms. Odd-shaped volcanic rocks covered in moss line the path which runs parallel to Centennial Walkway.

The path starts on the other side of the duck pond and rambles alongside its overflow, before looping back on Centennial Walkway where wizened trees arch over the trail – just asking to be climbed!

Let the kids loose to burn off some energy before heading home, or take some time to enjoy a picnic on the grassy slopes nearby.

INFORMATION

GRADE: Easiest

ACCESSIBILITY: Well-graded walkways in the glasshouses.

The quarry has steps and dirt paths.

TIME: 30 min.

FACILITIES: Museum, sculptures, drinking fountain, bike stands, toilets and café.

LOCATION: Multiple access points from Park Road, Grafton Road and Titoki Street.

Follow the car park signs within the Domain.

DOGS: On leads.

INFORMATION

GRADE: Easy

ACCESSIBILITY: Boardwalk, steps and dirt paths.

TIME: 20 min (about 500 m) return.

FACILITIES: Café, museum and toilets.

LOCATION: On the northern side of the Auckland Domain duck pond, by the café.

DOGS: On leads.

CENTRAL AUCKLAND

EPSOM | ONE TREE HILL
CORNWALL PARK

This sprawling urban park was gifted to New Zealand in the early 1900s and remains a popular spot for families and tourists to visit. Find a patch of greenery to relax on and watch the kids tear around, clamber over trees and peek at the cute farm animals.

The park was gifted to New Zealand by philanthropist Sir John Logan Campbell in 1901 and was named in honour of the Duke and Duchess of Cornwall and York, who were visiting New Zealand at the time.

An excellent spot to start your adventure is the Huia Lodge Discovery Hub, which has free maps of the park as well as interactive displays showing how the area would have looked during Māori settlement. While exploring, see if you can find the 150-year-old pōhutukawa or the small folly beside Twin Oak Drive.

In late September/early October the cherry blossoms draw the crowds – the most extensive collection is halfway down Pōhutukawa Drive when entering from Greenlane West.

ACACIA COTTAGE

Auckland's oldest-surviving wooden building was built by William Brown and his business partner Sir John Logan Campbell. While the outside was primarily Brown's work, the inside was meticulously completed by Campbell. It was built in downtown Auckland on O'Connell Street but was moved to its current location in 1920. Sit on the porch and imagine what life was like during the early 1900s. The cottage is opposite the Huia Lodge Discovery Hub.

THE FARM

This working farm has been operating since the 1920s and has approximately 600 sheep and 60 cows, and there are two full-time farmers who tend to the land and animals. Visit in lambing season to see the fluffy newborns. But please take care as young animals need time to settle in, and the park's team often creates restricted areas until the newborns are strong enough to be moved to more public spaces.

TRAIL MAPS

Visit the Cornwall Park website to download garden, exercise, kids, heritage and tree trail maps.

CENTRAL AUCKLAND

FIND OUT MORE
aucklandmtb.co.nz

GREY LYNN

ARCH HILL MTB PARK

This urban mountain bike park is just a stone's throw away from downtown Auckland.

More than three kilometres of trails snake through this small bush remnant close to the city. The trails range in grade from 'Training Wheels' for newly-minted MTB riders, to the more challenging gravity-driven 'Super Highway'! These trails were built by Auckland Council and are maintained by the Auckland Mountain Bike Club. So, grab your bike and attack this family-friendly park or contact the club to attend one of their regular events or working bees. There is no charge to ride here.

WHERE TO START?

From the end of Ivanhoe Road, walk up the concrete path, and you'll see the trail sign on the far right of the grassed area. Plenty of parking is available on the street.

TRAINING WHEELS

This trail is ideal for those just learning. It is a short single track that winds through the trees and has a fine gravel and dirt surface that creates a nice flow. This Grade 2 (Easy) trail is about 300 metres long.

IMPORTANT

- Always ride with a helmet.
- No walking on the trails.
- Stay in control, don't skid, cut corners or make new lines.
- Take all your rubbish home.
- Clean your bike to avoid spreading weeds.
- Have fun and be safe out there on the trails!

FIND OUT MORE
cornwallpark.co.nz

INFORMATION

GRADE: Easy/Medium/Hard

ACCESSIBILITY: Paved roads to rough dirt tracks – your choice!

TIME: Cornwall Park Loop Path – allow 40 min (about 3 km) return. Huia Lodge Discovery Hub to the summit of One Tree Hill – allow 30 min one way.

FACILITIES: Café, barbecues, toilets and drinking fountains. A playground by the Stardome Observatory.

LOCATION: Main entrance is off Greenlane West.

DOGS: On leads.

13

CENTRAL AUCKLAND

WATERVIEW
TE AUAUNGA | OAKLEY CREEK WALKWAY

Meander alongside the city's longest urban stream, which is surrounded by greenery teeming with native critters, to a picturesque waterfall.

The 50 hectares of green space beside the creek is home to plenty of native and exotic flora and fauna, even kākahi/freshwater mussels. Peer off the bridges – can you spot the threatened kūwharuwharu/longfin eel hiding? Follow the narrow concrete path upstream to the picturesque six-metre-high falls which look impressive after a downpour. Look out for the pīpīwharauroa/shining cuckoo, matuku moana/white-faced heron, tūī and mallard ducks along the way. Te Auaunga means 'swirling waters'.

Oakley Creek is approximately 15 kilometres long, which makes it the longest urban stream on the Auckland isthmus. It begins near Mount Roskill, before entering the Waitematā Harbour through the Motu Manawa/Pollen Island Marine Reserve.

WHERE TO START?

Waterview Reserve has a fantastic playground with plenty of parking. Follow the signs to the motorway overpass, and on the other side, the walkway entrance is on the left. The playground has toilets, barbecues, a splash pad, pump track and covered picnic shelters.

BEFORE YOU SWIM

Jump online to safeswim.org.nz and check the current water quality before taking a dip.

ALTERNATIVE ROUTE

Park at Phyllis Reserve and walk to the bushline where you'll see a steep concrete path leading down to the creek. At the junction turn right and walk approximately 10 minutes to the waterfall. This option includes steps.

INFORMATION

GRADE: Easy

ACCESSIBILITY: Outdoorsy buggies and bikes (be careful of walkers) will cope on the uneven concrete paths.

TIME: 1 hour (about 3 km) return. More for playground, paddling and picnics.

LOCATION: Waterview Reserve on Herdman Street.

DOGS: On leads.

FIND OUT MORE
oakleycreek.org.nz

CENTRAL AUCKLAND

EPSOM | ONE TREE HILL
MAUNGAKIEKIE | ONE TREE HILL

This prominent volcanic remnant was once the site of Auckland's largest Māori pā, which was home to nearly 5,000 people.

INFORMATION

GRADE: Easy/Medium

ACCESSIBILITY: Road

TIME: Allow 30 min (about 1.5 km) one way from the Hub; 15 min (about 600 m) return from the car park.

FACILITIES: Drinking fountains, ice cream shop, café, information centre and toilets.

LOCATION: Park at the Huia Lodge Discovery Hub at Cornwall Park (p12), or follow the road past the Hub to a smaller car park on the left.

DOGS: On leads.

Take a stroll to the summit and see the impact that the vast – and very impressive – Maungakiekie pā had on the surrounding landscape. The many terraces and pits used for homes, agriculture and defence are still visible.

The volcanic cone is about 180 metres high, and its scoria cones were created from the eruption of three craters – only one remains intact. Geologists estimate that it formed more than 28,500 years ago. It is the city's second-largest volcano – behind Rangitoto shimmering in the Hauraki Gulf.

The maunga/mountain was named after a single Monterey pine which stood on the summit until it was attacked in the 1990s, and later felled in 2000. Sixteen years later, a grove of tōtara and pōhutukawa was replanted on the summit. The band U2 famously immortalised the volcano in their hit song 'One Tree Hill'.

The 48-hectare domain adjoins Cornwall Park and creates a vast green space within the city. The summit obelisk was dedicated to Māori by Sir John Logan Campbell, who gifted the park to the people of New Zealand and is buried under the obelisk.

MĀORI NAME

Maungakiekie means 'the mountain where kiekie grows abundantly'. The native plant is a densely branched woody climber, and its sweet-tasting fruits were a delicacy for Māori.

PARKING

There is no parking at the summit, so you'll need to find a spot in the car park off Olive Grove. Or, just stroll from the Huia Lodge Discovery Hub. There are plenty of off-road tracks that snake up to the summit too.

ACCESSIBILITY

Contact Auckland Council for an access code to drive to the summit. Wheelchair users might need a helping hand due to the road's steady incline.

15

CENTRAL AUCKLAND

NEWMARKET | REMUERA
HOBSON BAY EAST PATH

This boardwalk winds through freshwater wetlands and saltmarshes to a circular concrete lookout with views across the pretty bay.

This short family-friendly adventure leads to the picturesque Wilson's Beach. The 1880s stately home above the beach – now part of Saint Kentigern Boys' School – was owned by the Wilson family.

Walk under the shady pōhutukawa trees until you reach the lookout which has views across Hobson Bay. Initially, the beach was open to the harbour but drainage works and the installation of a railway embankment has enclosed it – making it a fantastic sheltered spot for littlies to have a paddle.

The beach here was known to Māori as Tinana and Waitaramoa was the original name for the promontory overlooking the bay. Tinana was linked with a Ngāti Whātua chief who resided in the area.

The bay is valued for its kaimoana/seafood by the Ngāti Whātua Ōrākei community. Many species live here, including kahawai and karahū/sea snail.

TĪTIKO | MUDFLAT SNAIL

This mollusc lives in habitats between land and sea. It's not entirely land-dwelling, nor is it a marine snail. They are very common on tidal mudflats.

It has an operculum (gill cover) and breathes air, which is uncommon for snails with operculums.

Historically, mature-sized snails were plentiful; however, because they were hard to extract from their shells, they were not hugely popular to eat.

Image © Peter de Lange

16

CENTRAL AUCKLAND

PONSONBY
HUKANUI RESERVE | KELMARNA GARDENS

Combine these adventures into a fun outing, with a healthy dose of organic education in the mix too.

Hukanui Reserve is part of the larger Cox's Bay Reserve, and has a grassy knoll with towering pines and a wide boardwalk through mangroves. The entrance is just a couple of minutes' walk from Kelmarna Gardens, near the corner of Hukanui Road and Pārāwai Crescent (or at the far end of the gardens, over the stile). The walk loops back onto Pārāwai Crescent, so just keep turning left.

Opoutukeha/Cox's Creek was an early boundary between two iwi who collected flounder and shellfish near the headwaters.

KELMARNA GARDENS

This organic community garden has blooms galore and hearty vegetables growing across nearly two hectares of council land. Wander around the veggie plots and spot the bees and the worm farm. Most of the produce is available for purchase through the on-site shop.

ALTERNATIVE ROUTE

You can start from Victoria Avenue, although there's minimal parking and it includes a steep path. If you'd like to extend your adventure, the walk 'officially' includes Ōrākei Bay Village.

INFORMATION

GRADE: Easy

ACCESSIBILITY: Boardwalk and well-graded paths.

TIME: 30 min (about 1.5 km) return to the lookout.

LOCATION: Parking beside Martyn Wilson Field on Shore Road.

DOGS: On leads.

INFORMATION

GRADE: Easy

ACCESSIBILITY: Well-graded paths with one small flight of steps.

TIME: 30 min (about 1 km) return.

LOCATION: Entrance by 12 Hukanui Crescent for gardens.

DOGS: On leads.

CENTRAL AUCKLAND

MISSION BAY
KEPA BUSH PATH

This reserve is the second-largest patch of native bush on the Auckland isthmus, and it is home to an array of interesting critters and plants.

Boardwalk and gravel paths loop around this peaceful 14-hectare reserve which overlooks Purewa Creek. The plant life here has high ecological value, and seeds collected from the reserve play an essential role in regenerating East Auckland's 33-hectare Pourewa Reserve.

Listen out for tūī, kererū/New Zealand pigeons, riroriro/grey warblers, kōtare/sacred kingfishers and pīwakawaka/fantails which all help disperse native seeds through the forest. But they also drop pest plant seeds too.

Can you spot the 300-year-old kohekohe tree with its 3.2-metre circumference? This species was common within the coastal forest broadleaf forests that once covered the region. It's also an important source of nectar for birds just before the colder months in May and June.

Take some time to look in the small stream that runs beside the inner path, as banded kōkopu have been seen here. There are three known species of kōkopu in New Zealand; banded kōkopu, giant kōkopu and shortjaw kōkopu. Kōkopu juveniles are called whitebait. And if you're keen on an evening adventure, there are plenty of glow-worms to spot clinging to the damp forest banks.

The perimeter walk has vantage points over Purewa Creek to Purewa Cemetery, which is the resting place for more than 45,000 people.

Budding train enthusiasts may see an Eastern Line train trundle past.

IMPORTANT

It's worthwhile taking a photo of the map by the entrance as some of the paths can be confusing. Bring old shoes in winter as a small section of the trail becomes a fun muddy adventure.

INFORMATION

GRADE: Easy/Medium

ACCESSIBILITY: Dirt paths, boardwalk and steps.

TIME: 30 min (about 1.5 km) return for a quick explore.

FACILITIES: Picnic table by the entrance.

LOCATION: Thatcher Street.

DOGS: On leads.

CENTRAL AUCKLAND

STONEFIELDS
MAUNGAREI | MOUNT WELLINGTON

This maunga/mountain is the youngest on-shore volcano to have erupted on the Auckland isthmus. It arrived in a fiery blast approximately 9,000 years ago, and today its 135-metre cone offers views across the bustling city.

The eruption created a flattish rim with three craters which eventually became a settlement for Māori, who levelled out areas for their homes and gardens. You can still see the terraced pā sites and fortification ditches on the cone.

The paved road that winds up the dormant volcano is a popular exercising route, and although it is a steady climb, the distance is short enough for kids to tackle.

Allow 10 to 15 minutes to walk to the flat grassy area before a non-buggy-friendly side track heads up to the summit's trig with all-around views. The trig track can get muddy in winter.

Kids can tear up and down the steep grassed slopes which surround the central levelled area, while less energetic folk can relax at the picnic table. The crater is fenced off, but you can peer down into it and see a few exposed volcanic rocks.

There are views across the city, Waitematā Harbour and Rangitoto Island, and the nearby Maungarei Springs Wetland (p20) which was originally a quarry for the lava flow from Maungarei/Mount Wellington.

ACCESSIBILITY

If you have limited mobility, contact Auckland Council for an access code so you can drive to the top. Wheelchair users will probably need a helping push up the road.

INFORMATION

GRADE: Medium

ACCESSIBILITY: Grass, dirt path and well-graded road.

TIME: 45 min (about 2 km) return to trig.

FACILITIES: Toilets near the car park.

LOCATION: Car park on Mountain Road, Stonefields.

DOGS: On leads.

CENTRAL AUCKLAND

STONEFIELDS
MAUNGAREI SPRINGS WETLAND

The sound of rock crushing at this former quarry was once deafening but now it's a peaceful oasis with just the mellow chirps of native birds 'interrupting' the serenity.

Meander through the wetland and soak up views of Maungarei/Mount Wellington and the dramatic bluestone rock faces beneath Lunn Avenue, where you can occasionally spot rock climbers clambering up.

This wetland is a relatively short adventure, which makes it perfect for little ones finding their feet or those mastering two wheels.

Bring a few sausages to cook on the electric barbecue while you spend an afternoon here.

And, if you can't face the day without coffee, there's a café nearby on Stonefields Avenue.

HISTORY

Beneath the wetland is a basalt lava field which was created when Maungarei/Mount Wellington erupted approximately 9,000 years ago.

Quarrying began in 1936, and about 18 million cubic metres of basalt was excavated. The rock was used for roads and the Auckland airport runway.

Sixty-five years after the quarry opened, rock supply dwindled, and the quarry closed.

Now the five-hectare wetland plays an essential role in treating stormwater from the Stonefields urban development, to reduce algal blooms downstream and prevent the build-up of heavy metals.

EXTEND YOUR ADVENTURE

If there's more gas in the tank after completing the wetland loop, you can tackle the four-kilometre Stonefields Heritage Trail, which takes you right around the Stonefields precinct.

You can also choose to detour up Maungarei/Mount Wellington (p19) if the kids are agreeable.

The best spot to start from is on Tephra Boulevard. There's a mix of pavement, gravel, a set of stairs and a short steep section. Allow 45 minutes to complete the loop.

CENTRAL AUCKLAND

MĀORI NAME
Maungarei means 'watchful mountain' or 'mountain of Reipae'. Reipae was a Tainui princess who travelled on a kārearea/New Zealand falcon to Whangārei and eventually married a local chieftain.

INFORMATION

GRADE: Easy

ACCESSIBILITY: Dirt and concrete paths, and boardwalks.

TIME: 30 min (about 800 m) for a casual explore of the wetland.

FACILITIES: Toilets, drinking fountain, barbecues and picnic tables.

LOCATION: Parking on Tephra Boulevard, Stonefields.

DOGS: On leads.

MAUNGAREI | MOUNT WELLINGTON

21

CENTRAL AUCKLAND

WESTERN SPRINGS
TE TOKAROA | MEOLA REEF RESERVE

Perched on the city's longest lava flow, this reef jutting out into the Waitematā Harbour has a chequered history and even hides some intriguing skeletons beneath its grassy mounds.

About 75,000 years ago, Te Kōpuke/Tītīkōpuke/Mount Saint John erupted, and lava poured down its flanks into the Waitematā Harbour. Despite rising sea levels and erosion, this lava flow still extends an impressive two kilometres into the harbour and remains the longest basalt lava flow in the Auckland volcanic field.

Te Tokaroa, which means 'the long rock', was traditionally an essential food-gathering site for Māori who used it for fishing, shellfish collecting and also gathering flax, before the land was leased to farmers and used for quarrying during the 1870s.

It also became the dumping ground for residential and commercial waste from the 1930s until the late 1970s. Beneath the mounds are tonnes of residential organic waste, building waste and concrete, as well as some more unusual items including dead zoo animals.

Today, this unique geological feature has been transformed into a place for a relaxed stroll or a more adventurous exploration of the reef. The path leads to the headland where the grass meets the exposed reef. If you don't mind muddy shoes, you can clamber across at various points here. Or, look out for the wooden plank which offers a dry-feet option.

Explore the stands of saltmarsh and mangroves growing on the flow and look out for the matuku moana/white-faced herons that call this reef home. If you're lucky, you might spot an endangered reef heron.

There are plenty of picnic tables dotted around the headland to spread out a summer feast and enjoy a few hours soaking up the view.

Bring the pooch for the off-lead area near the headland.

IMPORTANT
Take care as you head further out onto the reef as there are razor-sharp rock oysters to navigate, and keep an eye on the incoming tide if you are near the reef tip.

CENTRAL AUCKLAND

INFORMATION

GRADE: Easy/Medium

ACCESSIBILITY: Gravel buggy-friendly paths on the headland but walking only on the reef.

TIME: 1 hour (about 2 km) return for an explore.

FACILITIES: Toilet and drinking fountain.

LOCATION: Small car park and plenty of on-road parking on Meola Road, Western Springs.

DOGS: On-lead through the reserve. Off-lead in the fenced area.

23

CENTRAL AUCKLAND

MOUNT EDEN
MAUNGAWHAU | MOUNT EDEN PATH

This volcanic cone offers a bite-sized adventure for little explorers, and from the summit there are impressive 360-degree views of the narrow isthmus that divides the Waitematā and Mānukau harbours.

Despite dozens of volcanoes dotted throughout Auckland, this gem stands out as a family-friendly favourite. It's the city's highest volcanic cone at 196 metres but its well-graded road makes winding your way up to the summit easy, and suitable for a buggy outing. Or, if you're feeling energetic, you can cycle to the top. Numerous side tracks lead to the summit if you want to explore 'free range' – just keep heading upwards; you can't get lost! From the car park near the base, take either road entrance as they connect in a loop around the top.

When the mountain blew its top about 15,000 years ago, it created an impressive symmetrical 50-metre-deep crater which is known as Te Ipu-a-Mataaho/'the bowl of Mataaho'. The cone once housed a traditional fortified Māori village/pā, and you can still see terraces and food storage pits.

MĀORI NAME
Maungawhau means 'mountain of the whau/cork tree'. This small, shrubby tree has extremely light wood traditionally used by Māori as fishing floats. The volcanic cone was later called Mount Eden after George Eden, the first Earl of Auckland.

SKY TOWER
From the summit, you'll spy the 328-metre-high tower, which dominates the inner-city skyline. It was completed in 1997 and is the 27th tallest tower in the world. It has a casino, skywalk, observation decks and dining options, and it houses Auckland's primary FM radio transmitter.

ACCESSIBILITY
Contact Auckland Council if you have limited mobility and would like to drive to the summit.

Bikers must keep to the sealed roads.

IMPORTANT
Please remain on the summit boardwalk and do not enter the crater as it is wāhi tapu/sacred to Māori.

24

FIND OUT MORE
geonet.org.nz

AUCKLAND VOLCANIC FIELD

The Auckland isthmus has been shaped by violent volcanic activity. Explosion craters, scoria cones and lava flows have created stark landscapes to explore, climb and peer into.

The Auckland Volcanic Field is monogenetic, which means the approximate 53 volcanoes within it have generally only erupted once, except for Rangitoto which repeatedly erupted about 600 years ago. There is no way to predict when or where the next bubble of magma will burst through the landscape to create a new volcano.

The field has produced colossal lava flows that cover a large strip of the Auckland isthmus. The longest lava flow runs from Te Kōpuke/Tītīkōpuke/Mount Saint John and ends at Te Tokaroa/Meola Reef (p22). More than 50 lava tubes have been discovered, including the 290-metre-long Wiri Lava Cave. There are nine GeoNet seismographs around Auckland that monitor seismic activity.

DIFFERENT TYPES OF ERUPTIONS

The volume of the magma bubble dictates the eruption's size and duration, which can range from a few weeks to several years. Water determines how violent the explosion will be. If basalt magma mixes with water in the right ratio (either seawater or groundwater), it creates very explosive activity which blows the magma apart and creates low rings of pyroclastic rock (called tuff) around a crater – such as Lake Pupuke and Ōrākei Basin. With less water contact, lava emerges less explosively and builds a volcanic cone of lava, scoria and tephra (rock fragments). Maungakiekie/One Tree Hill is an example of a volcanic cone.

WIRI LAVA CAVE

This is Auckland's longest-known lava cave and is part of Matukutūruru/Wiri Mountain volcano. The tube was formed by cooling lava through which hot lava continued to flow. The cave is internationally renowned for its rare lava stalactites and contains a 'Gothic'-arch-shaped cross-section. The volcano's scoria cone once reached 80 metres above sea level and was the site of a fortified Māori village/pā but the cone has since been quarried away. The cave is closed off to the public.

INFORMATION

GRADE: Easy/Medium

ACCESSIBILITY: Dirt paths, and concrete road with a steady incline.

TIME: 45 min (2 km) return walking on the road. More for free-range exploring.

FACILITIES: Toilets.

LOCATION: Main entrance and parking on Puhi Huia Road, off Mount Eden Road.

DOGS: On leads, except by the signposted off-lead areas.

25

CENTRAL AUCKLAND

REMUERA
ŌRĀKEI BASIN PATH

There are boardwalks galore for the kids to run along at this picturesque tidal lagoon – and a long winding bridge that snakes over an estuary between two forest remnants.

This lagoon was abruptly created during a volcanic explosion about 85,000 years ago. It was initially a deep freshwater lake, but at the end of the last ice age when the sea level rose, the volcanic maar (crater) ruptured and formed the tidal lagoon visible today.

It is a popular spot for water sports, and you may see Auckland Water Ski Club members zipping across the basin.

Starting from the car park at Ōrākei Basin West Reserve, the path follows the grassed verge, then disappears into patches of forest. Climb the steps behind the Club and then follow the signs across Lucerne Road before dipping down a private road to the cool humped estuary bridge. Continue back to the car park along the boardwalk that runs parallel with the train line.

Gate-closure time signs are by entrance. Also, take care on the road as it narrows near the car park.

VOLCANIC MAAR

A maar is created when groundwater or seawater mixes with basalt magma to produce a violent steam explosion. Overlying rock is crushed and launched straight up into the air, along with ash, water and steam. Then it falls directly back to the earth. The result of this impressive explosion forms a broad shallow crater (surrounded by a low ring of tephra deposits) which generally fills with groundwater to become a shallow lake. A maar can range in size from 60 metres to more than 8 kilometres across, with depths from 10 to 200 metres.

CENTRAL AUCKLAND

ST HELIERS
TE PANE O HOROIWI ACHILLES POINT

Fancy a mini-adventure you can drive to? This point has spectacular views of the Hauraki Gulf, for minimal effort!

Suspended above a rocky headland, this lookout offers postcard-worthy views of sandy bays and islands dotted throughout the gulf. On arrival, you are greeted by three traditional carved tōtara pou whenua (land marker posts) that reflect the Māori heritage of the headland. The monument commemorates the New Zealand-crewed HMNZS *Achilles* which assisted in defeating the legendary German battleship *Graf Spee* in 1939. The explosive eruption that created the nearby Glover Park also cloaked the cliffs above Gentlemens Bay to the right of the lookout with debris from its tuff ring. This can be seen eroding from the cliffs.

MĀORI NAME
Te Pane o Horoiwi means 'the head of Horoiwi' and was named after Chief Horoiwi, who arrived on the waka *Tainui*.

INFORMATION

GRADE: Easy

ACCESSIBILITY: Boardwalk, concrete and dirt paths. There are a couple of flights of steep stairs.

TIME: 45 min to 1 hour (about 3 km) for the loop.

FACILITIES: Nearest toilets at Ōrākei Bay Village.

LOCATION: Car park off Ōrākei Road, near Ōrākei Bay Village.

DOGS: On leads. Off-lead by the water ski club.

INFORMATION

GRADE: Easiest

ACCESSIBILITY: Well-graded concrete path and boardwalk.

TIME: 10 min return.

LOCATION: Parking at the end of Cliff Road, past St Heliers Bay.

DOGS: On leads.

NATURE DISCOVERY

WHAT LIVES IN
AUCKLAND'S LAKES?

There's plenty of activity happening just below the surface of the city's lakes. Native eels jostle for space with introduced fish including goldfish and perch, while rainbow and brown trout test the skills of anglers on Lake Pupuke.

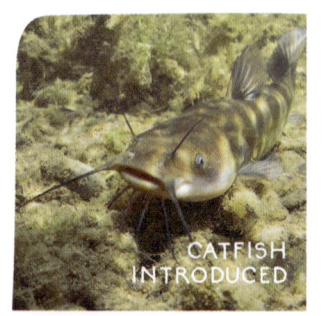

CATFISH INTRODUCED

RAINBOW TROUT – INTRODUCED

KŪWHARUWHARU NATIVE LONGFIN EEL

GOLDFISH – INTRODUCED

PERCH INTRODUCED

GAMBUSIA | MOSQUITOFISH – INTRODUCED

28

CENTRAL AUCKLAND

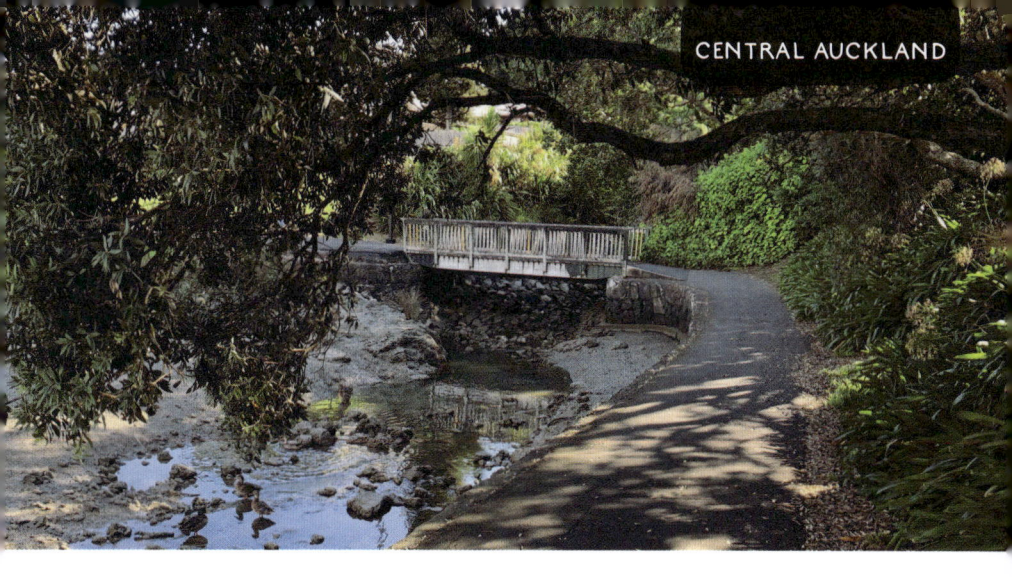

PANMURE
PANMURE BASIN PATH

This wide pathway loops around an extinct crater and is ideal for a family-friendly bike ride, or an easy stroll with the buggy. The city's youngest on-shore volcano, Maungarei/Mount Wellington (p19), overlooks the lagoon.

The basin isn't the most picturesque adventure when the tide is out but it is a pleasant enough urban adventure. However, on Sundays it gets much more entertaining with the opportunity to see miniature trains and boats.

The mostly flat walk looks better at high tide when the influx of water creates pretty reflections. There are good views of Maungarei/Mount Wellington, and you might spot a few waterskiers tearing across the water.

Look out for the protected kāruhiruhi/New Zealand pied shag near the Tāmaki Estuary bridge.

After meandering around the lagoon, hop on a train chugging along the Waipuna Miniature Railway which will delight train buffs of all ages. And you might see miniature boats on the nearby Scale Marine Modellers Auckland club pool. They sail most Sunday mornings from 10am until mid-afternoon.

INFORMATION

GRADE: Easiest

ACCESSIBILITY: Well-graded pathways.

TIME: About 40 min (3 km).

FACILITIES: Playground, toilets, fitness trail and skatepark.

LOCATION: Peterson Road, off Waipuna Road.

DOGS: On leads.

MINIATURE RAILWAY

Waipuna Miniature Railway trains run, weather permitting, every Sunday afternoon from 1pm to 4pm. The only exception is the two weekends over Christmas and New Year.

The railway is operated by Auckland Society of Model Engineers club volunteers.

Rides cost $2 each or $10 for six rides. Cash only.

FIND OUT MORE
asme.org.nz

CENTRAL AUCKLAND

GLEN INNES
TĀHUNA TŌREA NATURE RESERVE

The reserve is the perfect adventure for budding birdwatchers. Or if all things avian are not appealing, then the sandspit turns into an intrepid kid-friendly experience at low tide.

This magical landscape has plenty to entertain young explorers. Its 25 hectares has become a refuge for wildlife which inhabits the long sandbank that pokes out into the Tāmaki Estuary. Bring the binoculars and see if you can spot mallards, pūkeko, matuku moana/white-faced herons and kakīānau/black swans which live year-round in the wetland. Between November and March, the migratory wading birds return, including the gutsy kuaka/bar-tailed godwit that can fly up to 12,000 kilometres at one time. The best time for bird-spotting is between full tide and half tide.

The walk meanders from the car park through the bush to emerge on the long sandspit. Historically, this area was a vital kaimoana/seafood gathering site for Māori. The beach by the car park has excellent shady spots for a picnic or paddle, so bring the togs.

HIGHLIGHTS
Don't miss climbing to the top of the observation shelter, crossing

INFORMATION
GRADE: Easy/Medium

ACCESSIBILITY:
Well-graded paths, boardwalks, beach and sticky mudflats.

TIME: Allow 90 min (about 1.8 km) return for a leisurely explore, including sandspit.

LOCATION: At the end of West Tāmaki Road.

DOGS: No dogs allowed.

MATUKU MOANA WHITE-FACED HERON

Keep an eye out for these elegant birds which are often spotted stalking their dinner near shallow water.

They are quite tolerant of people walking nearby because they choose to feed near where humans hang out.

They're often spotted searching for dinner on damp sports grounds, estuaries and pasture.

They eat small critters including worms, insects and spiders, as well as little fish.

CENTRAL AUCKLAND

the weir and then at low tide exploring the Sandspit Beach Walk which creates a loop across exposed mudflats back to Cable Beacon Point. From there it's a short stroll back to the car park. Even at high tide – without the mudflats section – it's still a fun outing.

RONALD LOCKLEY

Welsh ornithologist and naturalist Ronald Lockley (1903-2000) founded the Tāhuna Tōrea Nature Reserve in 1975. Lockley immigrated to New Zealand in the 1970s and was a prolific author with more than 60 books to his credit. He was also a founder member of the Miranda Naturalists' Trust which established the country's first bird observatory on the Firth of Thames.

KUAKA | BAR-TAILED GODWIT

31

NATURE DISCOVERY

WETLANDS
FISH, BIRDS AND CRITTERS

These often elusive creatures thrive in Auckland wetlands. Good luck spotting a pūweto!

1. TAUHOU SILVEREYE/WAX-EYE

These friendly birds arrived by themselves in the 1800s and live throughout New Zealand in wetlands, forests and urban backyards. They are slightly smaller than a sparrow and are not considered endangered. They munch on insects, fruit and nectar. Tauhou means 'stranger' or, more literally, 'new arrival'.

2. PĀTEKE | BROWN TEAL

These endangered waterfowl were once common throughout the country but numbers have been in decline since the 1880s. With population estimates below 2,500, they are scarce and at risk of extinction due to predators and habitat loss. Pāteke have been spotted at Te Henga Wetland near Bethells Beach in West Auckland. Males have a green shiny head.

3. BLACK MUDFISH

These fish can survive out of water sometimes for months when their wetland dries out in summer. They burrow under tree roots or into the mud. They are found nowhere else in the world, which makes them pretty cool. They lower their metabolism into 'hibernation' mode until water returns, then they swim away! Image © Waikato Regional Council.

4. PŪWETO | SPOTLESS CRAKE

These mysterious birds are about half the size of a common blackbird and are so secretive they are hardly ever seen. They are common in the upper North Island, including at Te Henga Wetland. They build nests under the shelter of mānuka/New Zealand teatree and forage for food near shallow water under cover of dense raupō/bulrush or flax. They quickly hide when disturbed.

5. WEWEIA | NEW ZEALAND DABCHICKS

Māori named this bird after the sound of its occasional shrill call 'weeee-ee'. They anchor their nests to aquatic vegetation, which means the nests can be swamped by small rises in water level, especially boat wash. They are great divers (up to four metres) and can hold their breath for about 40 seconds.

6. NURSERY WEB SPIDER

This spider's webs are not for catching prey. Instead, they are little nurseries for young spiders. The female builds the nest when the young are about to emerge from the egg sac she carries during summer. The young nursery web spiders remain safe inside for about a week until they throw out a small thread to be caught by the wind – which is their way of 'leaving home'!

CENTRAL AUCKLAND

REMUERA
WAIATARUA RESERVE WETLAND LOOP

This urban wetland has plenty of space for adventurers to tear around on their bikes and explore within an impressive regenerating native wildlife refuge.

INFORMATION

GRADE: Easy

ACCESSIBILITY: Gravel and dirt paths.

TIME: 45 min to 1 hour (about 2.5 km) for the loop.

FACILITIES: Toilet, playground, basketball court and skatepark.

LOCATION: Grand Drive or beside the Remuera Golf Club on Abbotts Way.

DOGS: On leads. Off-lead areas available.

The path circles 16 hectares of restored wetlands within the reserve, and it's a popular destination for walkers, joggers, bikers and dog walkers who converge on the expansive green space.

It's the largest constructed urban wetland in the country but was originally a lake that formed after Maungarei/Mount Wellington (p19) erupted 9,000 years ago.

Now, after hundreds of hours of hard graft by volunteers and council staff, it is a reserve that provides year-round food supply for birds and insects that live in the wetlands, forests and meadows. It's also used to filter out sediment and other pollutants from the vast 674-hectare stormwater catchment area surrounding it.

There's a handful of viewing spots that take you deep into the wetlands where you might be able to spot kāhu/swamp harriers, pāpango/scaup (diving ducks), matuku moana/white-faced herons and pūkeko.

ACCESSIBILITY

The mainly gravel path is suitable for outdoorsy buggies but can get a little muddy in the middle of winter.

DOGS

This reserve has been voted as one of Auckland's best dog parks. It's mainly off-lead, although there are on-lead restrictions through the easily damaged wetland areas. During the weekend, there can be a large number of dogs roaming the park so best to avoid busy times if your kids are wary of dogs.

33

CENTRAL AUCKLAND

WESTMERE
WEONA-WESTMERE COASTAL WALKWAY

This impressive boardwalk winds through mangroves and pōhutukawa trees along the coastal fringe of Westmere – and has plenty of opportunities for some serious bird-twitching.

INFORMATION

GRADE: Easy

ACCESSIBILITY: Buggy-friendly out and back.

TIME: 1 hour (about 2.5 km) return from Lemington Road.

FACILITIES: Drinking fountain near Lemington Road entrance.

LOCATION: Easy access and plenty of parking near 40 Lemington Road.

DOGS: On leads.

The wide boardwalk passes through a significant ecological area teeming with native flora and fauna; pōhutukawa, nīkau, kōwhai and cabbage trees shroud the pathway.

And, if you slow down the pace, you'll probably sneak up on a few kōtare/sacred kingfishers perched on the railings eyeing up tasty morsels in the estuary beside Western Springs Creek.

With all the birdsong and views across to Te Tokaroa/Meola Reef (p22) and the Waitematā Harbour, this adventure feels isolated from the nearby bustling city – a slice of wilderness in the urban jungle.

After the boardwalk ends, the path does narrow a bit and becomes more undulating as it heads north to a small beach, and past cute boat sheds belonging to nearby residents. From here, there are steps up to Westmere Park Avenue.

HISTORY

Westmere was subdivided in the 1920s, and promotional

TARĀPUNGA
RED-BILLED GULL

It's not often you can enjoy fish and chips at the beach without these cheeky birds watching from the sidelines, eager to finish off your tasty morsels (although takeaways and bread are not great for their tummies).

These birds are kleptoparasites, which means they survive by stealing food from other animals – including humans!

It is the country's commonest gull and they are rarely found inland, except for a colony at Lake Rotorua.

34

CENTRAL AUCKLAND

material touted that a public reserve would be developed beside Motions Creek. But, over time, this coastal strip became overgrown, encroached on and lost as land for people to explore. In 2011, the community and council developed a plan for the area, and the walkway officially opened in 2016.

ACCESSIBILITY

There are a few access points to the reserve but not all are buggy-friendly. We started at the entrance near 40 Lemington Road, which suits buggies and wheelchairs.

If you don't mind steps, start from Meola Road through Lemington Reserve, or from Westmere Crescent.

Wheelchair users might want to turn around at the end of the boardwalk.

KŌTARE | SACRED KINGFISHER

NATURE DISCOVERY

BIRD WATCHING

WESTERN SPRINGS BIRD LIFE

How many of these birds can you see near the lake?

1. PŪKEKO | PURPLE SWAMP-HEN

Although they're not known for their elegant flying style, pūkeko can still fly long distances and are great swimmers. They mainly eat seeds, roots and shoots but will chomp down on passing spiders and insects as well. They are widespread, live in permanent social groups and will defend their territory aggressively.

2. CANADA GOOSE

These noisy birds give a loud honk when they're surprised. After they were introduced as a game bird into New Zealand in 1905, their population numbers exploded. By 1996, their estimated population had grown to 40,000 in the South Island, and the bird's protected status was removed in 2011. They like living near lakes or large ponds.

3. KAWAU PŪ | BLACK SHAG

These loners generally forage by themselves and are found from Northland to Bluff. They can weigh more than two kilograms, and no one is quite sure how many live in New Zealand; perhaps from 5,000 to 10,000 adults. They munch on mainly small to medium-sized fish – less than 35 centimetres in length – including spotties and smelt.

4. AUSTRALIAN COOT

These birds arrived by themselves from Australia and are considered a 'self-introduced' species, which means they are fully protected. They become very territorial during breeding between September and March, so try to avoid disturbing them. They like hanging out on the water and cruise around bobbing their little heads. When frightened, they seek shelter among the reeds.

5. MALLARD DUCK

It's such a Kiwi thing to do – head to the lake to feed the ducks! These introduced birds are probably the ones queuing to take your snacks. About 20 batches of mallards were imported in the 1870s, and now they are one of the most common fowl species in the country. They primarily eat plant material like seeds and grains. Don't feed them bread!

The males have a dark, iridescent-green head and bright yellow bill, while the females (and juveniles) are mottled brown with orange-and-brown bills.

6. KAKĪĀNAU | BLACK SWAN

These graceful birds tend to hang out in pairs, and during breeding will defend their pond patch or lake edge vigorously. They are common throughout New Zealand and mainly live on lakes and larger ponds, and some estuaries. When they fly or lift their wings, you can see their pure-white flight feathers.

36

CENTRAL AUCKLAND

WESTERN SPRINGS
WESTERN SPRINGS PATH

This wide, flat path loops around an urban bird sanctuary and is perfect for wrangling two buggies. So, grab a friend and go for a stroll or relax by the sprawling playground.

INFORMATION

GRADE: Easiest

ACCESSIBILITY: Wide concrete paths.

TIME: 30 min (about 1.8 km) return.

FACILITIES: Drinking fountain, public art, playground and toilets.

LOCATION: Great North Road, Western Springs. Parking on Motions Road.

DOGS: On leads.

This spring-fed lake was one of the city's earliest water sources and has become an urban wildlife sanctuary for an array of native and exotic birds. The lake is called Te Wai Ōrea, which means 'waters of the eel'.

It is home to the endangered native kūwharuwharu/longfin eel which grows at a glacial pace of between one and two centimetres each year. Peer over the picturesque humped red bridges and see if you can spot one of these remarkable creatures lurking in the shallows.

The main walking loop has wooden seats and picnic tables if you'd like to extend your visit. There are plenty of grassed areas to kick a ball around or challenge the family to a game of cricket. Nearby are the Auckland Zoo, and Museum of Transport and Technology (MOTAT) which regularly operates a tram around the park.

Don't miss the free Fukuoka Garden with its iconic tea pavilion, waterfall and pond.

KŪWHARUWHARU LONGFIN EEL

When eels reach between 25 and 80 years old, they travel 5,000 kilometres to breed and lay eggs in the subtropical Pacific Ocean, before dying.

Amazingly, their fertilised eggs drift using ocean currents to reach New Zealand in an epic journey that often takes about 15 months. They transform into glass eels and then elvers before navigating rivers, waterfalls and sometimes dams as they move upstream.

Fishing is prohibited at Western Springs.

FIND OUT MORE
longfineel.co.nz

37

WESTHAVEN BOARDWALK

CITY ADVENTURES

DISCOVER
CITY ADVENTURES

There are plenty of free adventures in the city so splish, splash or cycle your way through some of these kid-friendly gems hidden within Auckland's hustle and bustle.

HIGHLIGHTS

SWELTERING HOT? HEAD TO WATERVIEW RESERVE WITH THE BIKES AND TOGS TO TACKLE THE SPLASH PAD AND THE PUMP TRACK ALL IN ONE OUTING.

The kids won't get bored here! Littlies will love the water features while older kids can hoon around the bike tracks (p41).

IF YOU ARE AFTER AN EASY ADVENTURE IN THE SADDLE, DON'T MISS TOOTLING ALONG TĀMAKI DRIVE AND GRABBING AN ICE CREAM.

This out-and-back route provides some of the most leisurely cycling in Auckland (p45).

A GIANT BOARDGAME FOR THE KIDS! PLAY SNAKES AND LADDERS OVERLOOKING TĀMAKI RIVER.

Let the kids exhaust themselves zipping down the slides and dashing back up the ladders in this real-life boardgame (p44).

CITY ADVENTURES

COOL OFF IN SUMMER
SPLASH PADS IN THE CITY

Cooling off with the kids for free in the city is super easy. Here are our top picks for spots to make a splash this summer. Always remember to slip, slop, slap and wrap! The splash pads are usually operational between September and May.

CENTRAL CITY
MYERS PARK

This park is one of Auckland's oldest parks, and it's perched right in the middle of the city's hustle and bustle. The splash pad was built on the original Myers Park paddling pool and some of its historical features have been retained. It's a hidden gem in the city. Can you spot the inscribed poem by Hone Tuwhare about the taniwha Horotiu who lived in the old Waihorotiu Stream, which had its source in the Myers Park gully? There are plenty of shady tree groves to laze under during an afternoon while enjoying a picnic. Had enough of cooling off in the water? Head over to the playground where the kids can tear around under the towering bird and insect sculptures. There's a path for scooters and bikes through the park.

FACILITIES:
Playground, toilets and water tap.

LOCATION:
Greys Avenue, Central City.

GREY LYNN
GREY LYNN PADDLING POOL

You'll need to drag the kids away from here. This free paddling pool is open every day from early December to March and has a lifeguard to keep an eye on things. It's fully fenced so toddlers can't make a run for it while they learn essential water safety skills. It's shaded and shallow, and if you're not keen on hitting the beach, this is a perfect freshwater option. All dried off? Race over to the playground right next door to tackle the crowd-pleasing flying fox, swings, climbing frames, balancing log, fitness trail, skateboarding half-pipe and loads of gardens to explore. The pool is closed on Christmas Eve and Christmas Day.

FACILITIES:
Drinking fountains, picnic tables, toilets and cycling racks.

LOCATION:
Grosvenor Street or Williamson Avenue, Grey Lynn.

Image © Frances Chan

HOBSONVILLE POINT
CATALINA WATER PLAY PARK

Gather the troops for a lazy weekend outdoor barbecue at Hobsonville Point. This small water play park ticks all the boxes, and kids can use their imagination to direct water through wheels and channels to their heart's content. The park has a nice suburban feel to it and is worth a visit if you are in the area.

Have the kids run out of enthusiasm for pumping water? Head up to Harrier Point Park with its towering 10-metre-high kāruhiruhi/pied shag sculpture and slide, Te Kanohi O Te Manu. Be warned – it's a fast slide! There's plenty here to entertain all ages and you can finish off the day with an ice cream near Hobsonville Point Wharf.

FACILITIES:
Barbecues, drinking fountain, seating and shelter.

LOCATION:
Corner of Onekiritea and Tuatua Roads, Hobsonville Point.

CITY ADVENTURES

MĀNGERE
MOANA-NUI-A-KIWA OUTDOOR FUN POOL

Kids looking to perfect their bombing skills? Head to Māngere where there's a dedicated 2.6-metre-deep 'bombing pool'. Imagine how impressed all their mates will be when they nail the perfect mānu! There are five different-shaped pools here, an outdoor splash pad and hydro slides. Younger kids will have fun splashing around in the toddlers' pool. The outdoor pools are open during summer and are free for both adults and kids.

FACILITIES:
Changing rooms, toilets and leisure centre facilities.

LOCATION:
Mascot Avenue, Māngere.

Image © Auckland Council

MĀNU HINT: THE MORE BODY SURFACE THAT HITS THE WATER, THE BIGGER THE SPLASH!

MOUNT EDEN
POTTERS PARK SPLASH PAD

This was the city's first public splash pad, and its popularity continues to grow. During the weekends and school holidays, the park is teeming with families enjoying the colourful tip buckets, mini explosive jets, mists and fountains. Shady spots under the trees surround the splash pad, so you can settle in for a picnic and refuel the kids. It's the perfect suburban spot to cool off on sweltering summer days. There is a shared path around the park which is ideal for an after-dip bike ride. It's hard to miss the 5.6-metre-high 'Boy Walking' sculpture (Ronnie van Hout, 2019) depicting a larger-than-life child strolling. The land for Potters Park was donated by well-known Auckland philanthropist Frederick S Potter.

FACILITIES:
Basketball court, band rotunda, learn-to-ride track, picnic tables, barbecues and toilets.

LOCATION:
Corner of Dominion and Balmoral Roads, Mount Eden.

WATERVIEW
WATERVIEW RESERVE SPLASH PAD

Settle in for an afternoon at this beach-themed sprawling playground with its interactive water play area. There's something here for all ages. Littlies will love the fun splash pad, while older kids can graduate from tearing down the super-cool slides to tackling the pumping BMX track. Cool off during summer under the shelter when things get too hot and bring a picnic or sausages for the free barbecues. Nearby is the walkway to Te Auaunga/Oakley Creek Waterfall where you can walk beside the city's longest urban stream before taking a dip at the waterfall (p14).

FACILITIES:
Playground, basketball court, learn-to-ride track, beach volleyball, skateboard and scooter tracks, accessible toilets and barbecues.

LOCATION:
Herdman Street, Waterview.

CITY ADVENTURES

TWO-WHEEL EXPLORING
PUMP TRACKS AND BIKE PARKS

AVONDALE
AVONDALE LEARN-TO-RIDE TRACK
Tucked beside the Avondale Racecourse, this gem lets kids tootle around on their bikes following the cheerfully-coloured painted roads, take heed of the pedestrian crossings, bump their way over judder bars and navigate past other riders. This park has a relaxed community feel about it and provides good visibility of all kids.

ACCESSIBILITY:
Absolute beginners, learners on balance bikes and trainer wheels, confident riders on pedal bikes with trainer wheels, and scooter riders.

FACILITIES:
A playground and basketball courts. Toilet nearby on Great North Road (look for the giant spider).

LOCATION:
Car park off Racecourse Parade, Avondale.

BIRKENHEAD
BIRKENHEAD PUMP TRACK
With all the twists, turns and humps needed to keep riders of all ages busting out some moves, this reinforced concrete pump track and nearby dirt trail will please budding trail bikers. The sign recommends the path isn't for beginners, but it would suit kids on balance bikes at quiet times. Not suitable for scooters as they could 'bottom out' on top of the rises. This track has good visibility for keeping an eye on multiple kids.

ACCESSIBILITY:
Learners on balance bikes and trainer wheels, and confident riders on pedal bikes with trainer wheels.

FACILITIES:
A playground, skate park, toilets by the park entrance, changing rooms, high-ropes course, picnic tables and sports fields.

LOCATION:
Birkenhead War Memorial Park, Mahara Avenue, Birkenhead. Enter through the big gates, then drive to the end of the park.

FORREST HILL
GREVILLE RESERVE LEARN-TO-RIDE TRACK
Locals love this track — where else can kids cruise around on top of a large concrete reservoir? The road-map markings have faded over time but it's still ideal for kids transitioning to a pedal bike or for helping them to become more confident in an expansive space. There's plenty of room here to manoeuvre, although take care near the unfenced reservoir edges. The nearby MTB trail is suitable only for experienced older kids.

ACCESSIBILITY:
Absolute beginners, learners on balance bikes and trainer wheels, confident riders on pedal bikes with trainer wheels, and scooter riders.

FACILITIES:
Playground, skatepark, toilets, drinking fountain, sports fields and barbecues.

LOCATION:
Forrest Hill Road, Forrest Hill.

CITY ADVENTURES

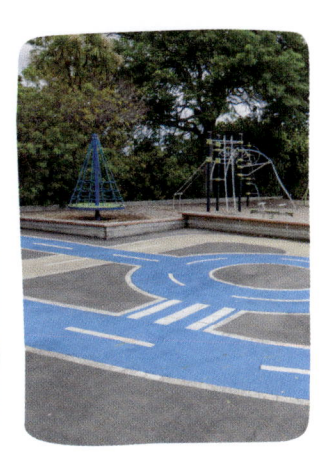

GREY LYNN
GREY LYNN PUMP TRACK

The track within the sprawling Grey Lynn Park has five 'lanes', which makes for fantastic long loops and plenty of variety. It's popular with the entire family – and the envy of plenty of other neighbourhoods – and all ages can get among the action with their balance bikes and trainer wheels through to the 'grown-up' BMX bikers and skateboarders. No scooters are allowed, and it's not suitable for absolute beginners. The sign suggests skill levels from novice riders onwards.

ACCESSIBILITY:
Learners on balance bikes and trainer wheels, confident riders on pedal bikes with trainer wheels, and scooter riders.

FACILITIES:
Drinking fountain, toilet, basketball court, exercise equipment, sports fields and an off-lead dog area.

LOCATION:
Dryden Street, Grey Lynn.

NORTHCOTE
ONEPOTO BEGINNER'S PATH

This family-friendly outing suits kids of all ages. The sealed cycling circuit has traffic markings, intersections to practise turning and giving way, and a roundabout. More confident kids can challenge themselves by navigating bridges, jumps, bumps and other fun obstacles. This park does draw the crowds so it might not be suitable during the weekend for kids wary of congested pathways. Once you've finished with the bike track and nearby playground, you can stroll along the pretty boardwalk within Onepoto Domain.

ACCESSIBILITY:
Absolute beginners, learners on balance bikes and trainer wheels, confident riders on pedal bikes with trainer wheels, and scooter riders.

FACILITIES:
Drinking fountain, playgrounds, sports fields, toilets and barbecues.

LOCATION:
Onepoto Domain, Tarahanga Street off Sylvan Avenue, Northcote.

PONSONBY
TOLE RESERVE RIDE TRACK

This teensy-tiny track suits small riders just starting. The painted road snakes around some curves and roundabouts and little kids will love the size, which is just right for them! After tearing around the streets, the playground right next door lets kids burn off some more energy. They might also be keen to watch the teenagers tackle the gnarly vintage skate bowl nearby. Locals' tip: bring a book to swap at the little pop-up library.

ACCESSIBILITY:
Absolute beginners, learners on balance bikes and trainer wheels, and scooter riders.

FACILITIES:
Skatepark, playground, drinking fountain. Toilets at the Ponsonby Community Centre on Ponsonby Terrace.

LOCATION:
Tole Street, Ponsonby.

Bike Auckland
www.bikeauckland.org.nz

CITY ADVENTURES

LET LOOSE ON THE
CITY'S PLAYGROUNDS

HENDERSON
TŪĪ GLEN RESERVE
Play among the treetops! This nature-themed playground has towering climbing nets, rope bridges, dual flying fox, eagle's nest swing and large tree huts. Perfect for engaging kids with heights in a safe environment.

LOCATION:
Claude Brookes Drive, Henderson.

PAKURANGA | FARM COVE
SNAKES AND LADDERS
A giant boardgame for the kids! Play snakes and ladders in real life by zooming down the slides and clambering back up the posts and ladders. This hillside park overlooks Tāmaki River and will tucker out even the hardiest kids.

LOCATION:
Bramley Drive, Farm Cove, Pakuranga.

WESTGATE
ROYAL RESERVE
WHOA! Let the kids race down a two-metre-wide hill slide before they tackle the custom-built towers. There are even areas for littlies to play – including sand pits – and a sprawling skills park for budding bikers to tear around.

LOCATION:
Beauchamp Drive, Westgate.

NORTH SHORE
TAKAPUNA BEACH
Let loose on this playground with its intertwining pipe slides and massive towers. There's plenty here, climbing nets to water-play areas. Things getting too hot? Bring your togs and jump into the surf which is just metres away from the playground.

LOCATION:
The Strand, Takapuna.

FREEMANS BAY
WESTERN PARK
A 25-metre-long slide! It's one of the longest and highest slides in the city. But if that's too scary, there are plenty of other things to burn off energy on at this colourful park, including treehouses, swings, a seesaw and a flying fox.

LOCATION:
Beresford Street West, Freemans Bay.

CITY ADVENTURES

EXPLORE ON TWO WHEELS
BIKE ADVENTURES

Discover adventures for kids on trainer wheels right through to experienced riders with more gas in the tank to tackle longer rides. Choose from vibrant-coloured mothballed motorway ramps to pedalling along the waterfront.

CENTRAL CITY
TĀMAKI DRIVE

Take a relaxed cycle along the waterfront from downtown Auckland to the quaint St Heliers Bay Village. This out-and-back route provides some of the most leisurely cycling in Auckland and, helpfully, is close to coffee and ice cream. If you work up a sweat – unlikely, because this cycleway is made for dawdling – jump into the Waitematā Harbour to cool off.

GRADE: Easiest

TIME: 1 to 2 hours return.

DISTANCE: 10 km one way or as short as you'd like.

FACILITIES: Toilets and cafés.

ACCESSIBILITY: Buggies, bikes and wheelchairs.

LOCATION: Numerous starting points along Tāmaki Drive or from the end of Queen Street.

DOGS: On leads.

CENTRAL CITY
TE ARA I WHITI THE LIGHTPATH

The mothballed Nelson Street off-ramp has been transformed into a vibrant pink pathway that snakes its way through the bustling metropolis. Are you visiting at night? Make sure that you look behind to see the interactive LED lights following you. This cycleway is a short, colourful fun adventure which kids on bikes and scooters will love.

GRADE: Easiest

TIME: 30 min return if you dawdle and take selfies.

DISTANCE: 700 m one way.

FACILITIES: Toilets and cafés.

ACCESSIBILITY: Buggies, bikes and wheelchairs.

START FROM: 1. The southern end of Nelson Street across Union Street to the pōhutukawa sculpture. 2. Near corner of East Street and Mercury Lane.

DOGS: On leads.

WESTHAVEN
WESTHAVEN BOARDWALK

This easy, flat ride for young riders snakes its way alongside the water's edge, beneath the Harbour Bridge to Silo Park with its excellent playground. There are plenty of spots to take a breather and the adventure is a mixture of boardwalk and small road sections. Do a little bit of yacht-spotting or grab a bite to eat at a café.

GRADE: Easiest

TIME: 80 min return.

DISTANCE: About 6 km return.

FACILITIES: Toilets and cafés.

ACCESSIBILITY: Buggies, bikes and wheelchairs.

START FROM: There is plenty of parking along Curran Street, or in one of the Westhaven Marina car parks.

DOGS: On leads.

TAKAPUNA REEF FOSSIL FOREST

NORTH AUCKLAND

EXPLORE
NORTH AUCKLAND

From spooky military tunnels within a dormant volcano to following in the historic footsteps of Māori who gathered kaimoana/seafood from the Waitematā Harbour, there's plenty to do north of the central city.

HIGHLIGHTS

KIDS WILL LOVE THE SOUND OF THE CARS RUMBLING PAST JUST METRES ABOVE THEM ON TŌTARATAHI | STOKES POINT RESERVE.

The Auckland Harbour Bridge dwarfs this small historic headland, which is the perfect spot for a quick adventure to escape cabin fever and stretch the legs (p49).

WHERE ELSE CAN YOU SEE BRIGHTLY PAINTED MUSHROOMS 'GROWING' ON THE TOP OF A MOUNTAIN?

Clamber all over Takarunga | Mount Victoria, which has a varied history – everything from a Māori pā/fortified village to a folk music club! (p59)

EXPLORE UNDERGROUND MILITARY TUNNELS, ROCK-HOP ALONG THE BEACH AND ROLL DOWN GRASSY BANKS.

Don't forget your torch to explore deep within grass-clad Maungauika | North Head Reserve (p56).

47

NORTH AUCKLAND

CHELSEA
CHELSEA ESTATE HERITAGE PARK

Wander along the paths that sugar workers returned home on after toiling in the iconic sugar refinery during the late 1800s.

Once you drive through the gates of this 37-hectare estate, the steep road passes five original brick homes that were built in 1886 to accommodate the refinery's factory workers. At the bottom, the impressive factory looms large. You can see why the road was used for a Downhill Derby with home-made carts in the 1970s!

In the early 1880s, a temporary shanty town of 60 tents was erected by the factory to accommodate the majority of the 150 workers while the factory was under construction. These men became the first to be offered jobs in the refinery, and about 100 signed up. The refinery became the biggest employer on the North Shore in the early 1900s.

WHERE TO START
The kid-friendly George Giles Walkway starts at the main car park beside the factory and heads over the small embankment towards the wooden boardwalk. Follow the path to Chelsea Bay Beach for an explore and paddle, then return to play on the little playground beside the factory. The car park gate closes at 8pm.

EXTEND YOUR ADVENTURE
The Chelsea Heritage Path starts from the car park and loops up Colonial Road to see the workers' cottages, then returns via the marked tracks through the reserve. Allow 30 minutes (about 2 km) return. The Bill Hayes sculpture was designed from a mechanical jaw that gathered an impressive 8.5 million tons of raw sugar during its working life.

INFORMATION

GRADE: Easy

ACCESSIBILITY: Well-graded dirt paths and boardwalk.

TIME: 45 min (700 m) return for the walk and playground.

FACILITIES: Café, playground and toilets.

LOCATION: End of Colonial Road, Northcote.

DOGS: On leads.

48

NORTH AUCKLAND

NORTHCOTE POINT
TŌTARATAHI | STOKES POINT RESERVE

The Auckland Harbour Bridge dwarfs this tiny historic headland, and kids will love standing beneath the bridge and hearing the cars rumbling past just metres above them.

This vantage point was occupied for many centuries and remnants of Te Ōnewa Pā can still be seen today. The boardwalk from the car park crosses the village's defensive ditch and leads to a waka-shaped pou whenua (land-marker post) that acknowledges the gods, future leaders and community. Māori who lived here enjoyed a rich diet including shellfish, berries, kūmara and fish – especially shark.

In the mid-1800s the site and surrounding area were purchased by the government and subdivided. The Auckland Harbour Bridge was built in the late 1950s and has overshadowed this historic site. There is a memorial plaque for three men who died during the bridge's construction.

The headland used to be more extensive but has shrunk in size due to erosion from water sluicing off the bridge while it was being cleaned.

MĀORI NAME
Te Ōnewa was the name given to the wider area, while the point itself was referred to as Tōtaratahi/one tōtara tree in 1908. The headland has also been called Point Rough, Stokes Point and Northcote Point.

EXTENDED ADVENTURE
Take the small footpath with steps down to Northcote Point Wharf for an alternative view of the bridge.

INFORMATION

GRADE: Easiest

ACCESSIBILITY: Boardwalk.

TIME: 15 min to soak up the city views.

FACILITIES: None.

LOCATION: Plenty of parking at the end of Princes Street, on Northcote Point.

DOGS: On leads.

49

NORTH AUCKLAND

ALBANY
LUCAS CREEK WATERFALL

Who doesn't love a pretty waterfall that is only minutes away from a pirate-themed flying fox surrounded by bush?

INFORMATION

GRADE: Easy

ACCESSIBILITY: Kell Park has full accessibility. The waterfall trail has gravel and steps.

TIME: 1 hour to combine the two adventures and for kids to fling themselves down the flying fox a few times.

FACILITIES: Toilets, playgrounds and cafés.

LOCATION: Kell Drive, off Dairy Flat Highway, Albany.

DOGS: On leads.

Kell Park is a lush urban green space that hides a flying fox and seating area where you can watch the kids exhaust themselves by launching off a wooden pirate ship down between towering trees.

Once they have had their fill here, you can walk along the wide boardwalk that winds through a small regenerating patch of forest. The path continues to Lucas Creek where there's a small viewing platform that's popular with anglers.

LUCAS CREEK WATERFALL

The Lucas Creek Waterfall is further upstream — so return to the car park and walk west on Dairy Flat Highway for a few minutes, before carefully crossing the road at The Albany. Behind the restaurant, you can access the new pathway that leads to Lucas Creek Waterfall.

This fan-shaped waterfall is impressive after rain but it's still worth a visit during the drier months to stretch the legs.

DANIEL LUCAS

The area around Albany was originally called Ōkahukura or Kaipatiki but was renamed Lucas Creek in 1845 after the mysterious flax trader Daniel Lucas. No one is sure where he came from, or when he arrived in New Zealand — and despite buying land beside the creek in the 1840s, he abandoned it in 1846 when he left Auckland. There is no record of him dying in New Zealand, so he may have left the country. The area was renamed Albany in 1890.

50

NORTH AUCKLAND

NARROW NECK
Ō PERETU | FORT TAKAPUNA

This fort's lofty position above the Hauraki Gulf was key to quelling the nation's unease in the late 1880s when Russia appeared to be threatening war with the British Empire.

INFORMATION

GRADE: Easy/Medium

ACCESSIBILITY: Paved paths, grassy slopes, steps and rocky shoreline.

TIME: 1 hour for an explore.

FACILITIES: Nearest toilets are at Narrow Neck Beach.

LOCATION: Gillespie Place off Vauxhall Road.

DOGS: No dogs on the reserve between 9am and 7pm from Labour Weekend to Easter Monday.

The fort was built between 1886 and 1889 and joined a chain of new defences swiftly constructed around Auckland Harbour including Maungauika/North Head Historic Reserve, Takaparawhā/Bastion Point, Point Resolution and later at Takarunga/Mount Victoria.

The fort consists of two main buildings, including the red brick barracks which housed soldiers and the smaller building where the warheads for torpedoes and depth charges were stored.

Historically, there was a dry moat that surrounded the buildings – that's why they are sunk into the ground. Most of the moat was filled in 100 years ago.

During WWI and WWII, the fort was a critical observation and defence post, accommodation for German prisoners of war, a hospital, and training ground for Māori and Cook Island reinforcements.

In 2000 the land was reclassified as a Historic and Recreation Reserve.

MĀORI HISTORY

Ō Peretu means 'the dwelling place of Peretu' and refers to Takapuna Head. The headland was home to a succession of tribes including people of Tainui and Kawerau descent. After several generations of warfare, the tribal groupings of Ngāti Whātua, Kawerau ā Maki and Ngāti Pāoa hold a cultural and spiritual connection to the headland.

WALKING TRAIL

While there isn't a formal walking path around this historic site – unless you follow the Toyota Kiwi Guardians trail on the next page – you can loosely loop around all the military relics in one hour, or let the kids explore free-range across the grassy areas.

IMPORTANT

Take care as there are steep drop-offs around the cliffs and some of the historic features. Keep an eye on the kids while they explore.

NORTH AUCKLAND

TOYOTA KIWI GUARDIANS
Ō PERETU | FORT TAKAPUNA

This area was once private Defence Force land, but today you can roam freely around the historic site. Watch the ferries whisk visitors around the harbour while you soak up the views. Discover some wonderful coastal treasures as you explore this unique military adventure.

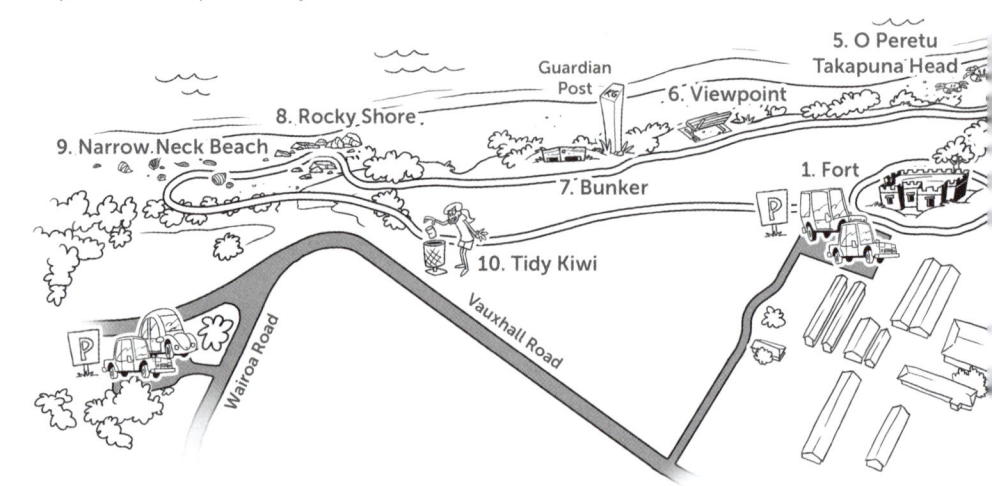

This adventure is part of the Toyota Kiwi Guardians programme. Before you visit, download an activity sheet from kiwiguardians.co.nz or use the one in this book. Claim a medal when you find the unique code written on the Kiwi Guardian Post.

1. MAIN FORT: A drawbridge, two huge guns and a moat used to surround this fort, just like a castle. Can you believe it was built way back in the 1880s?

2. ENGINE ROOM: Down the hill lies the old engine room. What do you see when you peer inside?

3. GUN SHELTER: Soldiers would spy on enemy ships from here. It's a great place to play 'I spy'.

4. SECRET PATH: Take the secret path to discover different creatures in the rock pools on the rocky shore. But make sure you watch your step!

5. Ō PERETU / TAKAPUNA HEAD: One reason this area is important to Māori is for its kaimoana. What sort of seafood do you think they would catch?

6. VIEWING POINT: Do you know that there are more than 15,000 different living things in our oceans? Many call Tīkapa Moana/Hauraki Gulf home. Whoa – that's a lot!

7. BUNKER: This tiny bunker was used by soldiers to spot enemies in Tīkapa Moana/Hauraki Gulf. Can you spot any ships or boats today?

8. ROCKY SHORE: Look at all the shells! Start collecting and see how many different ones you can find. But make sure you put back any rocks to protect the homes of marine life.

9. NARROW NECK BEACH: Use sticks, shells and anything else you can find on the beach to create a sand castle like Fort Takapuna.

10. TIDY KIWI: Being a Kiwi Guardian means looking after our special nature. If you see any rubbish, pick it up and put it in a rubbish bin before you leave the area!

Image and content courtesy of Toyota Kiwi Guardians.

NORTH AUCKLAND

TOYOTA KIWI GUARDIANS

4. Secret Path
3. Gun Shelter
2. Engine Room

INFORMATION

GRADE: Easy/Medium

ACCESSIBILITY: Paved paths, grassy slopes, steps and rocky shoreline.

TIME: 40 min (about 1 km) to complete.

FACILITIES: Nearest toilets are at Narrow Neck Beach.

LOCATION: Gillespie Place off Vauxhall Road, Narrow Neck.

DOGS: No dogs on the historic reserve between 9am and 7pm from Labour Weekend to Easter Monday.

SAINT LEONARDS BEACH

53

NORTH AUCKLAND

LITTLE SHOAL BAY
WAI MANAWA | LE ROYS BUSH

Follow in the footsteps of Māori who traditionally used this well-trodden trail through the valley and former estuary to gather kaimoana/seafood from Waitematā Harbour.

Enter the bush reserve opposite Little Shoal Bay — don't forget to clean your shoes of kauri dieback disease. Can you spot any tuna/eels in the Dudding Park Stream? Further upstream is home to spawning īnanga/whitebait.

The estuary once ran a long way up the valley but after the mouth was constricted by waste dumped from the Auckland Harbour Bridge construction, the raupō/bulrush began to flourish and it became the second-largest wetland of its kind on the North Shore. On a windy day, listen to the rustling of the swamp plant.

The valley in Wai Manawa/Le Roys Bush was the route Māori traditionally followed to source food from Little Shoal Bay, including pipi and fish.

Look out for the waterfall halfway up the valley, then grab an ice cream where the trail ends at the Birkenhead shops before walking back through the urban bush-clad valley.

INFORMATION

GRADE: Easy/Medium

ACCESSIBILITY: Steps, dirt paths and boardwalk.

TIME: 60 min (about 4 km) return.

FACILITIES: Playground and toilets.

LOCATION: Council Terrace, Little Shoal Bay, Northcote Point.

DOGS: On leads.

ĪNANGA | WHITEBAIT

This small native fish, with its silvery belly, is found in coastal rivers, wetlands and lakes throughout New Zealand. Īnanga migrate downstream between February and May to lay eggs in dense vegetation flooded by spring tides. The eggs are stranded when the water retreats, hatching at the next spring tide before heading out to sea and munching on plankton for six months. During their return, while migrating back up streams, they are called whitebait — the most commonly caught of the six whitebait species found in New Zealand.

54

NORTH AUCKLAND

FIND OUT MORE
leroysbush.nz

Avid plant collector Edward Le Roy purchased the upper valley in 1918. The Forest and Bird Society (with assistance from local government) bought it in 1947, then the North Shore Scenic Board took it over eight years later.

Wai Manawa means 'the source of the water' and refers to the area being basin-shaped.

LITTLE SHOAL BAY RESERVE

This bay is a family-friendly spot to end your adventure and tucker out the kids with a high-tide dip. Pōhutukawa frame views across the bay and, at low tide, kids can walk on the mudflats to find aquatic critters. There are electric barbecues to cook up a hearty snack, and the sprawling playground has shade covers for sun protection.

KAURI DIEBACK

An upper section of the trail was closed at the time of writing. For an up-to-date map, visit the Friends of Le Roys Bush website.

Right image © Aimee Palmer

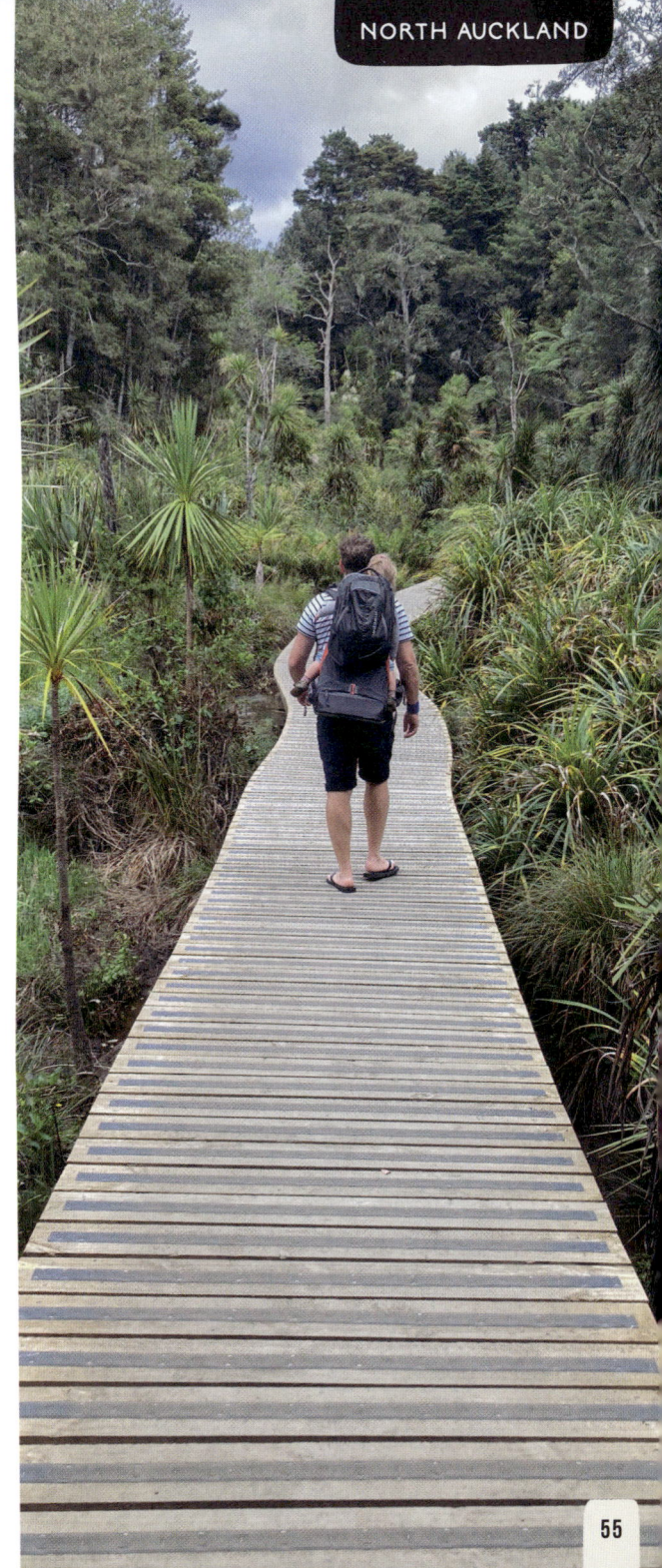

NORTH AUCKLAND

DEVONPORT
MAUNGAUIKA | NORTH HEAD HISTORIC RESERVE

Explore a maze of spooky military tunnels, rock-hop along the beach and roll down grassy banks. Bring a torch and head underground into this dormant volcano which erupted about 50,000 years ago.

INFORMATION

GRADE: Easy/Medium

ACCESSIBILITY: Paths, grassy slopes and steps.

TIME: Allow 1 hour to explore.

FACILITIES: Toilets.

LOCATION: Parking at the end of Takarunga Road.

DOGS: On leads.

Some rumours suggest deep within the hidden tunnels there could be anything from decaying ammunition to two original Boeing aeroplanes! Unfortunately, these mysterious claims remain unproven – although they make exploring the tunnels more fun. Who knows what you will find?

The reserve's strategic location at the entrance to Auckland's harbour was crucial during the country's coast defence era, which spans nearly 120 years of military history.

FORMER PĀ

But before that, Maungauika, 'the mountain of Uika', was an important site for Māori due to its rich volcanic soils and nearby kaimoana/seafood resources. Although it wasn't the main fortified settlement in Devonport, which was at nearby Takarunga/ Mount Victoria, the volcano's lower slopes were used for gardens and fish-drying racks.

MILITARY HISTORY

A pilot station was established here to guide ships into the harbour shortly after the settlement of Auckland in 1840. But from the 1870s, with the impending threat of a Russian invasion making the government twitchy, three large gun batteries were quickly built on the site. However, due to the haste of when they were built during the 'Russian Scares', they needed significant reconstruction to make them usable.

The Russians never invaded, and for 25 years dozens of prisoners were kept busy rebuilding the fortifications. During this time, most of the tunnels, searchlights and underground spaces – including the engine rooms and magazines – were built also.

The army departed North Head when the coast defence system was wound up by the end of the 1950s, and the

56

NORTH AUCKLAND

land became a reserve in the Hauraki Gulf Marine Park.

SOUTH BATTERY

One of the world's last 8-inch (about 20-centimetre) disappearing guns can still be spotted at South Battery, which faces over the inner harbour. The hefty barrels alone weighed more than 12 tonnes, and when fired, the recoil forced the gun to retract underground where it could safely be reloaded before reappearing to take another shot.

IMPORTANT

Take care as there are holes, sudden drops and plenty of uneven surfaces on this reserve – especially in the tunnels.

Dogs are allowed on lead at the reserve but the beach has separate rules. Visit Auckland Council's website for more information.

57

NORTH AUCKLAND

TOYOTA KIWI GUARDIANS
MAUNGAUIKA | NORTH HEAD HISTORIC RESERVE

This is an important historical site, but it's also a fantastic place to explore. There are forts with interlinking tunnels, spooky caves, massive old guns, trees to climb, hills to run down — it's got everything!

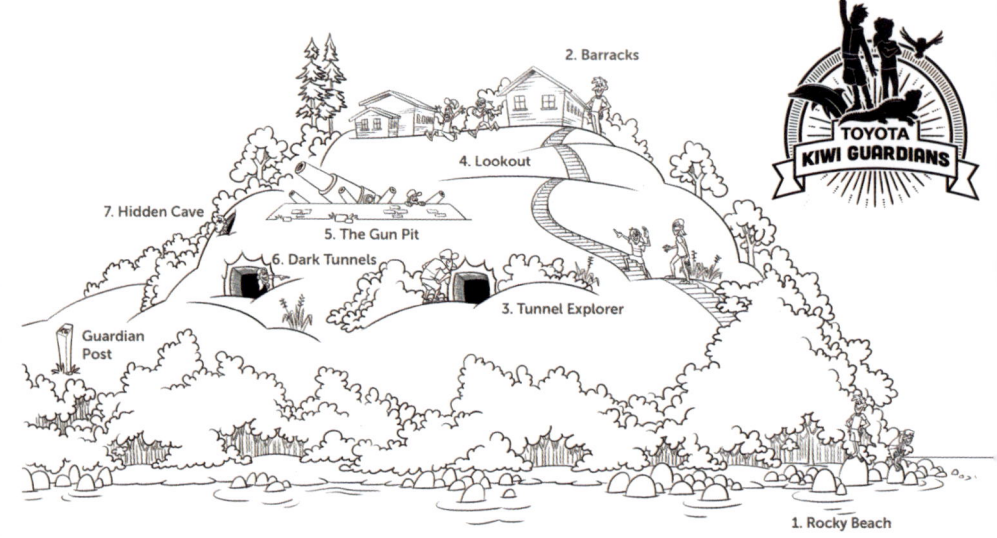

Map features:
- 1. Rocky Beach
- 2. Barracks
- 3. Tunnel Explorer
- 4. Lookout
- 5. The Gun Pit
- 6. Dark Tunnels
- 7. Hidden Cave
- Guardian Post

TOYOTA KIWI GUARDIANS

This adventure is part of the Toyota Kiwi Guardians programme. Before you visit, download an activity sheet from kiwiguardians.co.nz or use the one in this book. Claim a medal when you find the unique code written on the Kiwi Guardian Post.

This is a free-range adventure, so choose your own path. A torch is helpful for the tunnels.

Image and content courtesy of Toyota Kiwi Guardians.

1. THE ROCKY BEACH

2. HISTORIC BARRACKS:
Soldiers once lived here.

3. TUNNEL EXPLORER

4. THE LOOKOUT.
How far can you see?

5. THE GUN PIT.
Boom!

6. WHERE DO THE DARK TUNNELS LEAD?

7. THE HIDDEN CAVE.
What's in it?

INFORMATION

GRADE: Easy/Medium

ACCESSIBILITY: Paved paths, grassy slopes, steps and rocky shorelines.

TIME: Allow 30 min (about 1 km) for the adventure.

FACILITIES: Toilets.

LOCATION: Parking at the end of Takarunga Road.

DOGS: See page 57.

NORTH AUCKLAND

DEVONPORT
TAKARUNGA | MOUNT VICTORIA

This mountain has had a varied history – being everything from a pā/fortified village to a military outpost – and is now home to a folk music club.

Follow the summit road up the volcanic cone, past the Signalman's House. This vantage point informed locals about ship movements, as many Devonport homes were built with a direct line of sight to this building. Today, it houses the Michael King Writers Centre, which promotes New Zealand literature.

Take a short side trip to the Bunker and see if members of the Devonport Folk Music Club are belting out any tunes.

After reaching the summit, relax on the grassy knoll and watch the ships arriving and departing. This is the North Shore's highest volcano at 87 metres and was occupied by successive Māori iwi. You can still see the pā terraces and kūmara storage pits on the volcano's north-eastern slopes.

MĀORI NAME
Takarunga means 'the hill standing above' and the mountain's European namesake is Queen Victoria.

MUSHROOMS
The colourful mushrooms? They are vents for a water pumping station just beneath the surface of the maunga/mountain.

MILITARY HISTORY
Because of its location and height, the volcano was used as a military observation and control post. There are plenty of signs that give you an insight into its history as a fort. Don't miss climbing down the stairs to check out the Disappearing Gun. The weapon has only been used a handful of times, including a test firing which cracked windows in nearby homes. Locals were not amused.

VEHICLE ACCESS
Parking is available on nearby streets. There is a teeny car park beside the gate.

If you have limited mobility, contact Auckland Council for an access code so you can drive to the top.

INFORMATION

GRADE: Easy/Medium

ACCESSIBILITY: Well-graded road. Steps to the Disappearing Gun.

TIME: 45 min (about 1 km) return to the summit.

LOCATION: Parking on Kerr Street to access Mount Victoria Summit Road.

DOGS: On leads.

59

NATURE DISCOVERY

FOREST FLOOR DWELLERS
DISCOVER FUNGI IN AUCKLAND'S FORESTS

Fungi are pretty amazing things. They live on dark, damp forest floors and don't need sunlight to grow because they don't use light energy to fuel themselves. There are about 7,300 identified species of fungi in New Zealand.

TOOTHED JELLY FUNGUS

BRACKET/SHELF FUNGUS

PARUWHATITIRI | BASKET FUNGUS

YELLOW WAX-GILL FUNGUS

WEREWERE-KŌKAKO | BLUE MUSHROOM

NORTH AUCKLAND

WAIMAUKU | WOODHILL
WOODHILL FOREST MTB PARK

This purpose-built park has more than 80 kilometres of world-class trails. It's the country's largest mountain bike park and has everything you need for a family adventure. Bonus: it's only 40 minutes from Auckland.

The park provides a great introduction to mountain biking, with easy and scenic trails that you can pedal along at your own pace. The rolling terrain suits newbies wanting to get stuck in and kids just wanting to enjoy a relaxing ride in the forest with family and friends. You'll need to purchase a pass to use the park.

NATURE VALLEY TRAIL

This 6 kilometre Grade 2 (Easy) ride takes in different beginner trails. It was designed to give newly-minted riders a taste of riding on forest trails. The terrain is undulating with one main hill climb up a forest road.

It starts from the car park, around the family loop, up the hill to Map Station 1, using the road. A fun descent on the Over and Out trail brings you back to the car park.

HOW TO GET THERE

Turn off the North-Western Motorway and follow SH16 towards Helensville. Approximately 5 minutes past Waimauku turn left onto Restall Road. Follow the signs for about 1 kilometre.

NEED TO HIRE A BIKE?

Bikes are available from the pro shop, which is open year-round from 8am to 5.30pm, and on Wednesdays from 8am to 9pm. However, bikes need to be hired at least one hour before closing. It's best to book in advance to ensure the right size and style of bike is available.

The pro shop is closed Christmas Day and New Year's Day.

FIND OUT MORE
bikeparks.co.nz

INFORMATION

WHAT FACILITIES ARE IN THE PARK? There's a pro shop for advice and hiring/fixing bikes and a café that operates when the pro shop is open. Toilets are available.

WHEN IS THE PARK OPEN? The forest is open year-round except Christmas Day and New Year's Day, from 8am (weekdays) and 7am (weekends) to 5.30pm and on Wednesdays until 9pm.

HOW MUCH DOES IT COST TO RIDE IN THE PARK? Day, concession or season passes are required to use the park.

ARE E-BIKES ALLOWED ON THE TRAIL? Yes.

ARE DOGS ALLOWED ON THE TRAIL? Dogs are only allowed during the week and not on weekends or public holidays.

DOES THE FOREST CLOSE IN WINTER? No.

NORTH AUCKLAND

RIVERHEAD
RIVERHEAD FOREST MTB PARK

This privately-owned forest is a great location for some two-wheeled action through regenerating pine forest just 30 minutes from downtown Auckland.

The free-to-ride park provides sensational summer riding for families. It's the perfect spot to escape the city and whip up some pine needles while gaining more confidence on mountain bikes.

In 2006 West Coast Riders Club secured a large area of land within the forest for exclusive mountain bike use. Since then, passionate club members have built a quality trail network of more than 15 kilometres to suit most abilities.

The trails loop alongside the central Main Climb gravel access trail, so there are a couple of spots to bail if the going gets too gnarly.

The road takes you to the top of a ridge where you can choose your route down. Most of the trails are graded intermediate to advanced.

In winter, the clay-based pine forest can become slippery, so unless you have confident young free-wheelers, tag this adventure for the warmer months.

GAMBLER TRAIL

For younger kids, try the more accessible intermediate Gambler trail. This 700-metre single track is primarily downhill and is a popular option for confident riders who are graduating from easier routes. There are plenty of excellent flows,

WEST COAST RIDERS CLUB

Keen to earn some trail karma? Join the not-for-profit West Coast Riders Club, whose members are dedicated to building cool jumps and trails throughout Riverhead Forest.

Find out more about joining or lending a hand on the tracks at their website.

FIND OUT MORE
westcoastridersclub.org.nz

NORTH AUCKLAND

and it has good grip in summer, but it can get a little boggy in winter. Head up Main Climb, and you can connect with the start of the trail on the left off Smoker.

PUMP TRACK

Don't miss jumping on the pump track near the park's entrance (walk up Main Climb for a couple of minutes). Littlies on balance bikes through to adults regularly tackle the rollers and berms here. It's been built for flow, and there are a few gap jumps to test out everyone's mettle.

INFORMATION

WHAT FACILITIES ARE IN THE PARK? No toilets.

IS THERE TRAIL SIGNAGE? There is a map board just inside the park's entrance. Also visit Trailforks website.

WHEN IS THE PARK OPEN? The trails are accessible 24 hours.

HOW MUCH DOES IT COST TO RIDE IN THE PARK? It's free entry, but a donation to the West Coast Riders Club, whose members maintain the trails, is always appreciated.

ARE E-BIKES ALLOWED ON THE TRAIL? Yes. Please follow trail directions.

ARE DOGS ALLOWED ON THE TRAIL? Yes, but they need to be kept under control.

DOES THE FOREST CLOSE IN WINTER? No; but the trails do get muddy in the middle of winter.

HOW TO GET THERE From Auckland take SH16 out west, before turning off onto Old North Road. Drive 6 km north to the entrance on the left. Parking is beside the road. Allow 30 minutes (30 km) from downtown Auckland.

PĀREMOREMO
SANDERS RESERVE

This purpose-built park has more than 22 kilometres of twisty single-track mountain bike trails suitable for most skill levels, and a dedicated 500-metre-long mountain bike circuit for younger riders. The two options make this a great family MTB adventure.

The easy mountain bike trail beside the car park has been specifically designed for younger riders with small, achievable challenges to help them gain confidence on dirt trails. There's plenty of big picnic tables nearby, from where adults can keep an eye on the kids while soaking up the views towards Herald Island – make a day of it and bring a picnic. It's an ideal introduction to handling berms and fun rollers. More adventurous trails wind through this 41-hectare park perched on a small headland in the upper Waitematā Harbour, near Pāremoremo. There's a mix of wide open fast trails to tight twisty sections through the regenerating coastal forest. Bring long pants for the kids as the trails are mainly gravel.

There is a playground, toilets and changing rooms, car park, BMX and walking tracks, horse-riding areas, picnic tables and seating, drinking fountains and barbecues near the car park. Don't miss the Seat of Life and Faraway Tree sculptures near Library Point.

Dogs are required to be on a lead around the communal areas. There's an off-lead area for dogs near the park's entrance.

GETTING THERE

Head north on SH1 and exit at Greville Road. Drive through Albany Village, take the turn towards Pāremoremo, turn left onto Merewhira Road, and follow the signs from there. Allow about 30 minutes from downtown Auckland.

Every leaf just looks the same?

Not any longer.

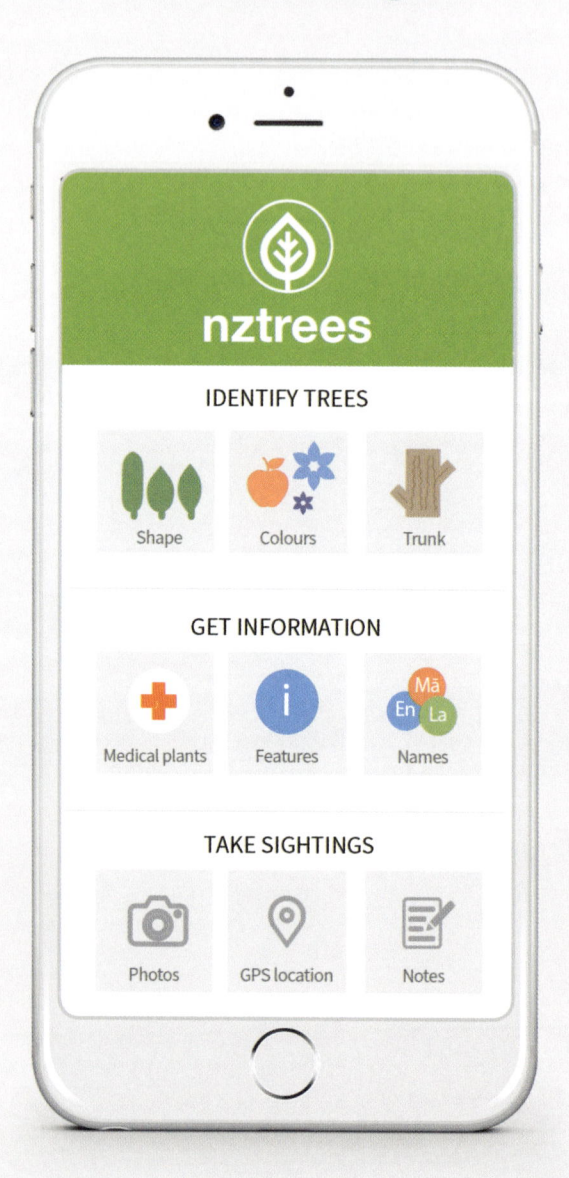

Download the NZ Trees app and familiarise yourself with the native tree species surrounding you. Collect your own sightings and share them with friends. Because you can only protect what you know.

Available from the Google Play and Apple App Stores.

REGIONAL PARKS

FAMILY-FRIENDLY PARK ADVENTURES
AUCKLAND REGIONAL PARKS

Make a day of it and explore one of the region's many protected parks. They have fantastic kid-friendly facilities, with some offering overnight camping. For more information and excellent trail maps, visit: aucklandcouncil.govt.nz

DUDER REGIONAL PARK

This coastal farm is perched on the Whakakaiwhara Peninsula and has spectacular coastal views. Visit in spring to spy plenty of cute lambs bouncing around, although throughout the year it is always rewarding to explore the peninsula. The park has a rich Māori history which stretches back to the 1300s when the famous *Tainui* canoe visited.

GRADE: Easy/Medium. Walking and cycle trails available.

DISTANCES: From 30 min to a few hours.

FACILITIES: Picnic spots, camping ground, orienteering and toilets.

DOGS: No dogs allowed.

LOCATION: From the central city, head south on SH1, turn off at Manurewa and follow the signs to Clevedon. Then follow North Road to the park.

LONG BAY REGIONAL PARK

Bring the togs, snorkels and kayaks to explore this sweeping beach which has loads to entertain the family. This accessible marine reserve is an excellent all-ages outing. Let the kids loose on the flying fox, jump around in the surf or take a sedate stroll along the nature trail.

GRADE: Easy/Medium

DISTANCES: From 30 min for the Nature Trail to a few hours.

FACILITIES: Picnic spots, electric and wood barbecues, camping area, playground, café kiosk, changing room, toilets and showers.

DOGS: Various spots for taking the pooch. Check the Auckland Council website.

LOCATION: From the central city, head north on SH1 for about 20 min. Turn off at Oteha Valley Road and follow the signs to Long Bay.

SHAKESPEAR REGIONAL PARK

This wildlife sanctuary has sheltered bays for swimming and plenty of trails to indulge in some bird spotting. There's so much to see – everything from wetlands through to a WWII gun emplacement. Lots of threatened native wildlife live within the sanctuary's almost 2-kilometre-long pest-proof fence.

GRADE: Easy/Medium. Walking and cycle trails available.

DISTANCES: From 30 min for the Kanuka Track, to a few hours.

FACILITIES: Picnic spots, camping ground, changing room and toilets.

DOGS: No dogs allowed.

LOCATION: From the central city, head north on SH1 for 30 min and turn off at Silverdale, then follow to end of the Whangaparāoa Peninsula.

MORE INFORMATION:
sossi.org.nz

ROTOROA ISLAND

HAURAKI GULF

SET SAIL ON THE
HAURAKI GULF

This turquoise-coloured gulf is peppered with ferries and recreational boaties throughout the year. And, from far beneath its ocean surface, volcanoes have erupted – one just 600 years ago! Set sail to discover idyllic islands so close to the city.

HIGHLIGHTS

CLIMB THE COUNTRY'S YOUNGEST VOLCANO AND EXPLORE THE WORLD'S LARGEST PŌHUTUKAWA FOREST ON RANGITOTO ISLAND.

Don't miss clambering through the dark lava tunnels or checking out the lush Kidney Fern Grove (p70).

DISCOVER HOW THE NATION'S FIRST ADDICTION CENTRE HAS BEEN TRANSFORMED INTO A WILDLIFE SANCTUARY ON ROTOROA ISLAND.

Take a stroll around this historic island and keep an eye out for takahē which happily roam wild here (p72).

BECOME AN EXPLORER ON KAWAU ISLAND AND FOLLOW THE TOYOTA KIWI GUARDIANS ACTIVITY TRAIL.

Take a dip at Ladys Bay and along the way, can you spy a wallaby or two? (p76)

HAURAKI GULF

TĪKAPA MOANA | HAURAKI GULF
RANGITOTO ISLAND

This iconic landmark is the nation's youngest volcano and was formed during a series of eruptions only 600 years ago. At the time, the adjoining Motutapu Island was settled by Ngāi Tai iwi who observed the fiery explosions that shaped the volcano — a fossil human footprint was discovered in ash layers on Motutapu Island!

The world's largest pōhutukawa forest grows wild on the flanks of this 260-metre-high volcano and creates an impressive explosion of crimson flowers during summer. A restoration programme on the 2311-hectare island has created a pest-free haven for native flora and fauna, including more than 200 species of moss, plants and trees. You'll see plenty of bait stations as you climb through the scoria fields and pōhutukawa forest. The island's main attraction is the summit, which involves a steady uphill climb. Don't miss taking a short detour to clamber through intriguing lava caves; these are doable with a phone torch but a head-torch makes for more comfortable hands-free adventuring. On your return, if you have time to fritter away while waiting for the ferry, there's a handful of kid-friendly short walks by the wharf to explore.

BACHES
Baches have been on Rangitoto Island since the 1920s. Most are privately owned, but a few are bookable by the public.

BACH 38 MUSEUM
If this cute bach is open, make sure to visit. You'll probably feel quite nostalgic at the iconic Kiwi décor! Peek inside the pantry and see if you sampled similar wares during your childhood. Entry is free but a donation helps maintain the baches.

MĀORI NAME
Rangitoto means 'bloody sky'. The island is known as Te Rangi-i-totongia-aī-te-ihu-o-Tamatekapua, which has been translated to mean 'the day that Tamatekapua had a bloody nose'. Hawaiki, born Tamatekapua, was the captain of the voyaging *Te Arawa* canoe and had a stoush with *Tainui* canoe captain Hoturoa, apparently over alleged adultery. Tamatekapua received a bloody and bruised face.

FIND OUT MORE
rangitoto.org

HAURAKI GULF

INFORMATION

GRADE: Medium/Hard

ACCESSIBILITY: There are a variety of surfaces from well-graded dirt paths to ankle-jiggling scoria. Only accessible for walking, so pop little ones in backpacks.

Limited accessibility? Private companies offer 4WD road-train tours on the island.

TIME: Allow a half day to explore. Four hours is plenty to summit the island and explore the lava caves and walks near the wharf.

For the keen, you could do it in less but a half day is relaxed for families.

FACILITIES: Toilets and shelter by the wharf.

FOOD OUTLETS: Bring plenty of water and snacks. There are no shops on the island.

RUBBISH: Pack out all your rubbish, including food scraps.

GETTING THERE: Less than 30 min by ferry from the Downtown Ferry Terminal.

DOGS: No dogs allowed on the island.

AUCKLAND PARKING: Close parking at the Downtown Car Park on Customs Street.

HAURAKI GULF

EXTEND YOUR ADVENTURE

Motutapu Island is connected to Rangitoto Island by a causeway which allows you to walk between the two islands. Visit doc.govt.nz for more information on exploring both islands in one day.

ESSENTIAL GEAR TO BRING

Conditions on the island can change quickly, so expect all seasons in one day. It can get chilly on the ferry ride too.

- Boots or shoes with a bit of a tread. No jandals.
- Togs and a towel during the warmer months.
- Torch for the caves.
- Sunglasses, hat, sunscreen and lip balm.
- Plenty of snacks and drinks for everyone.
- An extra warm layer and rain or wind jacket just in case.

SUMMIT TRACK

Climb through a pōhutukawa forest and past extensive exposed lava fields to arrive at a vantage point overlooking the city and Hauraki Gulf. There are plenty of seats here to relax and enjoy your snacks.

Unless you are keen, skip the summit rim walk as it doesn't add any significant thrills to your adventure. Instead, save your energy for the lava caves, which will delight the kids.

ACCESSIBILITY:
Medium grade. Uneven surfaces and steps.

TIME:
2 hours (7 km) return.

LAVA CAVES TRACK

The cooling of flowing lava created this dark tunnel, and adventurous kids will love heading underground and exploring the moss-covered rocks.

There's a splash of sunlight in the middle section but bring a torch as it's dark and there are plenty of uneven surfaces and rocks for kids to scrape their knees on.

ACCESSIBILITY:
Medium grade. Dark, uneven surfaces and some narrow spots.

TIME:
30 min (1.5 km) return off the Summit Track.

SHORT WALKS NEAR THE WHARF

The **KIDNEY FERN GLEN** (30 min return) is an untamed little adventure for kids through translucent kidney ferns (which look their best after rain) and moss-covered boulders. The **KŌWHAI GROVE** (30 min return) is a shady respite in summer and worth a trip when the kōwhai are in bloom. The zigzag **MANGROVE BOARDWALK** (5 min at a stretch) takes you briefly through mangroves to arrive at an archway that 'convicts' built as a grand entrance to toilets that now don't exist. They also constructed the nearby saltwater pools. Or enjoy a coastal walk to **FLAX POINT** (1 hour return) to visit a karoro/black-backed gull colony.

NATURE DISCOVERY

NATIVE TREES
TRUNKS AND BARKS

Sometimes you can't see the tops of towering trees poking through the forest canopy. So instead of getting a kink in your neck, here are a few different trunks and bark patterns to look out for – everything from flaky and stringy, to trunks that look like someone has dented them with a hammer!

1. TŌTARA
The trunk has thick, stringy, reddish-grey bark that peels off in long strips.

2. KAURI
The trunk looks like it has hammer marks on it, and leaks gum.

3. RIMU
The drooping, flaky bark has a deep red colour.

4. NĪKAU PALM
The trunk has circular grey-green scars where fronds have fallen off.

5. PONGA | SILVER FERN
White undersides on the fronds, and sometimes dead frond 'skirts' around the upper trunk.

6. PŌHUTUKAWA
Usually grows as a multitrunked spreading tree. The bark is rough and stringy.

71

HAURAKI GULF

TĪKAPA MOANA | HAURAKI GULF
ROTOROA ISLAND

This historic landmark in the Hauraki Gulf was closed to the public for more than 100 years while it housed the nation's first addiction treatment centre. But now, this wildlife sanctuary is an island refuge for some of New Zealand's rarest birds.

At 80 hectares the island is small enough to explore in a day but large enough that you won't run out of things to do or see.

You might spot free-roaming takahē going about their daily life! The first breeding pair was released on the island in 2015, and since then three takahē chicks have been successfully bred and transferred back to their habitat in Fiordland to keep the population growing, hopefully. But you can often spot another breeding pair – Mulgrew and Fyffe (left) – hanging out on the northern part of the island.

Rotoroa Island has four sprawling ecosystems: grasslands, forest, coast and wetlands. These can be discovered by exploring two of the main pathways on the island: the North Tower Loop Track and the Southern Loop Track.

After expending some energy exploring the island, you can while away an afternoon swimming in the turquoise water of the secluded coves dotted around the island. The best family-friendly swimming spots are Ladies' Bay, Men's Bay, Cable Bay and Mai Mai Bay.

Don't miss visiting the island's heritage buildings, including the original jail and 1860s schoolhouse to get a glimpse of what life was like on the island. The Kiwi woolshed-inspired museum and exhibition showcases the island's intriguing Māori and early European history.

HISTORY

The Salvation Army opened Rotoroa Island as a rehabilitation facility for alcoholics in 1911. It became the nation's first and longest-running addiction treatment centre. The facility served more than 12,000 New Zealanders before being disestablished in 2005. During this time, the island was mostly self-sufficient and covered in vegetable gardens, working farms and sprawling orchards. Four years after the Sallies left the island, the Rotoroa Island Trust

FIND OUT MORE
rotoroa.org.nz

HAURAKI GULF

was established and purchased a 99-year lease from The Salvation Army. Since then partners and volunteers have worked tirelessly to restore the island into a wildlife sanctuary and have so far planted more than 300,000 native trees.

GUIDED WALKS

Rotoroa Rangers regularly host 90-minute guided nature tours on the island to give visitors an insight into the island's natural history and ongoing restoration projects. Hopefully, you'll get to spot some of the island's avian residents too, including weka/woodhen, tīeke/saddleback, takahē and pāteke/brown teal. Then, after the tour, you are free to explore on your own. The tour is suitable for all fitness levels – although it might be a bit long for little kids.

ACCESSIBILITY

All the paths on the island are well-graded loose gravel but some are only suitable for outdoorsy buggies. You can explore Ladies' Bay (left) and the Men's Bay wetlands but going further afield will be up to how intrepid you feel because it does get pretty steep down to Cable Bay. The central part of the island from the wharf in Home Bay to Ladies' Bay is mostly flat, so this gives reasonably easy access to a fabulous safe swimming beach, grassland areas and the island's small museum and a nearby accessible public toilet. For wheelchair users, visit the island's website for accessibility information.

HOME BAY TRACK

This 10-minute stroll from the wharf takes you to the island's main facilities including the accommodation, toilets and museum.

The path follows the edge of the sprawling Home Bay which offers excellent picnic spots and is a picturesque anchorage for boaties.

Listen out for tīeke/saddleback in the pōhutukawa trees along the way.

NORTH TOWER LOOP TRACK

Keen to see all the kid-friendly sights? This 45-minute loop from the Exhibition Centre takes in some crowd-pleasing highlights: pristine white-sand beaches, regenerating wetlands, dense native forest and views across the Hauraki Gulf. The loop provides the best chance to see a mix of wildlife happily roaming around this offshore sanctuary. From here, you can extend your walk to explore further into the northern part of the island.

SOUTHERN LOOP TRACK

For older kids, this 90-minute hike is the longest on the island and is a bit more challenging than the North Tower Loop Track. Bring some sturdy shoes. It takes in some large-scale restoration planting areas and Chris Booth's sculpture, *Kaitiaki*, on the island's southern headland. The wind-bent branches of nearby pōhutukawa trees inspired the sculpture. Don't forget your togs as you'll pass Men's Bay, which is the perfect spot for a dip to cool off.

73

HAURAKI GULF

INFORMATION

GRADE: Easy/Medium

ACCESSIBILITY: The paths are loose gravel. No bikes allowed on the island.

TIME: One day to explore.

FACILITIES: Electric barbecues, toilets, drinking fountain and changing sheds.

FOOD OUTLETS: Bring plenty of water and snacks. Apart from a small kiosk offering snacks, there are no shops on the island. Food must be sealed in bags or containers due to the island's predator-free status.

RUBBISH: Pack out all your rubbish, including leftovers.

GETTING THERE: It's about 1 hour from Auckland with Fullers360 ferries. Private boats are welcome too.

DOGS: No dogs allowed.

STAY OVERNIGHT: If you're keen to experience the island's birdsong at dawn, then there are a few options to stay overnight — from hostel-style accommodation through to holiday homes. No camping is allowed. Book through the website.

ECO-TRAIL GUIDE: Keen to brush up on your flora and fauna identification skills? Grab a copy of the island's ecosystem guide from the Exhibition Centre so you can identify native birds and plants while you stroll around the island's different ecosystems.

NATURE DISCOVERY

BY THE COAST
DISCOVER SHOREBIRDS

How many of these cool birds can you spot hanging around Auckland's beaches and rocky shorelines?

1. POAKA | PIED STILT
These dainty wading birds are widespread at wetlands and coastal areas. They have slender necks and long legs, which helps them feed in deep water. They are a self-introduced species and arrived from Australia around 1800. They are notorious tricksters at distracting enemies from their nest and will fake injury or even death.

2. TARĀPUKA | BLACK-BILLED GULL
Although similar looking to the red-billed gull, the tarāpuka is more slender and has a longer bill. They are quite shy and generally mind their own business. Unfortunately introduced predators like cats and stoats means this gull – which is native to New Zealand – has become one of the world's most threatened gull species.

3. TŪTURIWHATU | NEW ZEALAND DOTTEREL
These endangered native birds build their nests above the high-tide mark on the beach, which unfortunately is close to where human activity occurs. Their camouflaged nests and eggs can be destroyed by vehicles or horses on the beach. They are monogamous (having only one partner at a time)

and can vigorously defend their territory.

4. KŌTUKU-NGUTUPAPA ROYAL SPOONBILL
The first royal spoonbill was recorded in 1861 at Castlepoint on the Wairarapa coast, and the first breeding was recorded in Ōkārito (Westland) in 1949. They often feed in shallow wetlands, alone or in small flocks. Watch as they submerge their bill and sweep it side to side to feed. The adults develop long white plumes on the back of their heads.

5. TŌREA | VARIABLE OYSTERCATCHER
These coastal waders are very protective parents and can aggressively dive-bomb to defend

their chicks. They are often spotted busily probing around on beaches and estuaries looking for shellfish. They open mussels and cockles by inserting their bill tip into the shell rim and twisting, or by hammering.

6. TAKAHIKARE-RARO NEW ZEALAND STORM PETREL
Thought to be extinct since 1850, birdwatchers spotted this fast-flying petrel in 2003 off the coast of Whitianga. But it wasn't until a decade later, after multiple capture programmes, that breeding burrows were discovered beneath the forest on Hauturu/Little Barrier Island. The small primarily dark blackish-brown bird has a white belly with dark streaks and white patches beneath its wings.

75

HAURAKI GULF

TĪKAPA MOANA
HAURAKI GULF MARINE PARK

The Hauraki Gulf Marine Park is home to a multitude of picturesque islands, with some now entirely pest free. These sanctuaries have allowed an incredibly diverse range of flora and fauna to flourish, so jump on a ferry and start exploring the Gulf's treasures!

KAWAU ISLAND HISTORIC RESERVE

In the mid-1800s, this island was home to a bustling copper mining settlement. Historical remnants remain on the island for kids to explore. Peek inside the impressive Mansion House, before venturing along the island's family-friendly walks – with many taking less than 1 hour. Or, bring the togs and wallow in the shallows while enjoying a day away from the city.

GRADE: Easy/Medium. Walking tracks only. No bikes, buggies or wheelchairs.

TIME: Walks from 10 min.

FACILITIES: Toilets, electric barbecue and café (during summer).

DOGS: No dogs allowed.

GETTING THERE: From Sandspit Wharf, near Warkworth, about 1 hour north of Auckland.

MORE INFORMATION: kawauisland.org doc.govt.nz

TIRITIRI MATANGI ISLAND

Spot some of the country's rarest birds while exploring this pest-free island. A network of trails winds past the country's oldest lighthouse still in operation, and through a variety of landscapes including beaches to laze on and lush coastal forests. Visit the Visitor Centre to learn how volunteers are protecting this wildlife sanctuary. Supporters of Tiritiri Matangi host guided tours which you can book at the same time as your ferry ticket.

GRADE: Easy/Medium. Mainly walking tracks. Very limited buggy and wheelchair access.

TIME: Walks from 30 min to 4 hours.

FACILITIES: Toilets. No food outlets.

DOGS: No dogs allowed.

GETTING THERE: 80-min ferry ride from Auckland. Allow a full day.

MORE INFORMATION: tiritirimatangi.org.nz

MOTUTAPU ISLAND

Volunteers have been replanting native trees and eradicating pests on this ancient island since 1994. Walking trails traverse the diverse landscape which includes wetlands, farmland and regenerating bush. Remnants of the 178-million-year-old island's varied history are still visible – from Māori occupation to sprawling Victorian picnic parties for more than 10,000 partygoers, and WWII relics.

GRADE: Easy/Hard. Walking tracks only. No bikes, buggies or wheelchairs.

TIME: Walks from 30 min to 4 hours.

FACILITIES: Toilets at Home Bay. Tent sites. No food outlets.

DOGS: No dogs allowed.

GETTING THERE: 35-min ferry ride from Auckland. Allow a full day.

MORE INFORMATION: motutapu.org.nz

HAURAKI GULF

TOYOTA KIWI GUARDIANS
KAWAU ISLAND HISTORIC RESERVE

This unique island paradise is packed with fun for the whole family! Take in the fantastic views, enjoy a stroll through the forest, relax on the beach, try to spot a wallaby, explore the historic Mansion House or enjoy a break at the café.

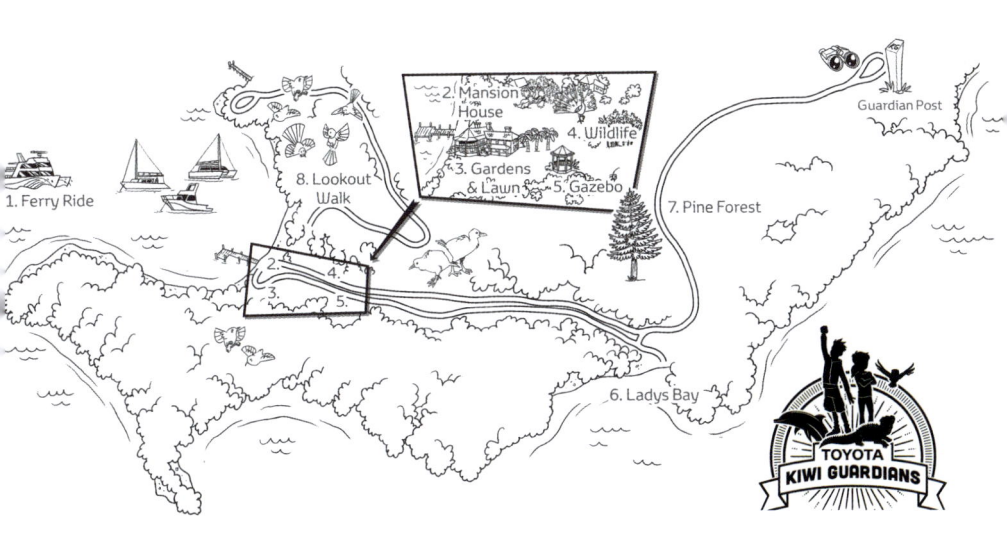

This adventure is part of the Toyota Kiwi Guardians programme. Before you visit, download an activity sheet from kiwiguardians.co.nz or use the one in this book. Claim a medal when you find the unique code written on the Kiwi Guardian Post.

Allow 1 hour 30 min for the 3 km loop. More details on page 76.

1. FERRY RIDE: Can you spot any seabirds? If you look closely, you might even be able to spot a dolphin or penguin.

2. MANSION HOUSE: Go back in time to the 1800s. What's your favourite part of the house?

3. GARDENS AND LAWN: Look at all the plants and trees in the garden. Can you tell which ones are native (from New Zealand) and which are exotic (from overseas)?

4. WILDLIFE: Keep an eye out for the beautiful pīkake/peacock and weka/woodhen. Did you manage to see any?

5. GAZEBO FACT-FINDING: Do you know what 'Kawau' means in te reo Māori? It's hidden somewhere – can you find it?

6. LADYS BAY: This used to be a popular ladies-only swimming spot. What special features do you notice about this beach?

7. PINE FOREST: While you walk along the track, look for wooden sculptures. You may see a wallaby. How might wallabies impact the forest?

8. LOOKOUT WALK: Walk to the lookout. What can you hear? What can you see? Can you see an island shaped like a beehive? Can you guess what it's called?

Image and content courtesy of Toyota Kiwi Guardians.

77

HAURAKI GULF

TOYOTA KIWI GUARDIANS
TIRITIRI MATANGI ISLAND

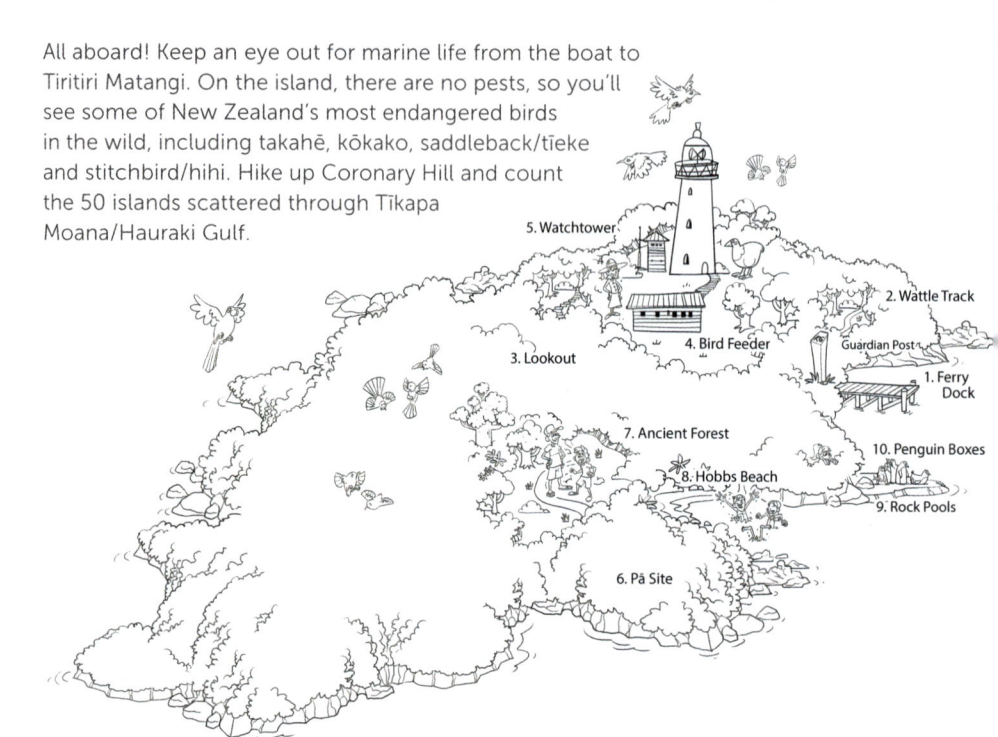

All aboard! Keep an eye out for marine life from the boat to Tiritiri Matangi. On the island, there are no pests, so you'll see some of New Zealand's most endangered birds in the wild, including takahē, kōkako, saddleback/tīeke and stitchbird/hihi. Hike up Coronary Hill and count the 50 islands scattered through Tīkapa Moana/Hauraki Gulf.

1. Ferry Dock
2. Wattle Track
3. Lookout
4. Bird Feeder
5. Watchtower
6. Pā Site
7. Ancient Forest
8. Hobbs Beach
9. Rock Pools
10. Penguin Boxes

This adventure is part of the Toyota Kiwi Guardians programme. Before you visit, download an activity sheet from kiwiguardians.co.nz or use the one in this book. Claim a medal when you find the unique code written on the Kiwi Guardian Post.

1. FERRY DOCK: Look for seabirds from the ferry – can you identify any?

2. WATTLE TRACK: This trail is bird central! Who will you spot?

3. LOOKOUT: Walk to the top of Coronary Hill. Can you see where you came from?

4. BIRD FEEDER: Watch who comes to visit the sugarwater feeder.

5. WATCHTOWER: Climb the stairs of the watchtower. The view is amazing!

6. PĀ SITE: Visit the Tiritiri Matangi Pā site and imagine what it was like to live here hundreds of years ago.

7. ANCIENT FOREST: Discover the ancient coastal forest.

8. HOBBS BEACH: Visiting in the summer? Take a refreshing dip at Hobbs Beach.

9. ROCK POOLS: Low tide? Check out the sea creatures in the rock pools.

10. PENGUIN BOXES: Quietly quietly lift the lid. Any penguins home?

Image and content courtesy of Toyota Kiwi Guardians.

TOYOTA KIWI GUARDIANS

VISIT THE NATION'S OLDEST OPERATING LIGHTHOUSE HERE!

INFORMATION

GRADE: Easy/Medium

ACCESSIBILITY: Walking only.

TIME: Allow 2 hours (3.5km) to complete.

GETTING THERE: It's 4 km off the coast of Whangaparāoa Peninsula, north of Auckland. You'll need to take a ferry from Central Auckland or Gulf Harbour (see p76).

DOGS: No dogs.

TE NAUPATA | MUSICK POINT

EAST AUCKLAND

EXPLORE
EAST AUCKLAND

Jump in the car and head east for adventures on sprawling dams hidden deep within the Hūnua Ranges, or to Maraetai Beach with its pretty white beaches and kilometres of kid-friendly cycleways.

HIGHLIGHTS

WALK TO A HISTORIC ISLAND WHICH IS ACCESSIBLE ONLY AT LOW TIDE.

Tantalisingly perched at the end of a shell bank with cockles hiding in the shallows, Motukaraka | Flat Island is worth spending half a day exploring to learn about its tragic past (p85).

JOIN THE CROWDS ADMIRING THE 30-METRE-HIGH HŪNUA FALLS AT HŪNUA RANGES REGIONAL PARK

Bring a picnic and hang out by this bush-shrouded waterfall which plunges off a volcanic basalt cliff. Don't miss the nearby walks for a longer adventure (p91).

KIDS NOT SCARED OF HEIGHTS? THEN THEY'LL LOVE THIS ADVENTURE AT TE NAUPATA | MUSICK POINT!

At low tide, clamber down the steep, steep steps that end on a dramatic headland with exposed rocks reaching out into the Hauraki Gulf (p82).

81

EAST AUCKLAND

BUCKLANDS BEACH
TE NAUPATA | MUSICK POINT

Visit at low tide and clamber down the steep staircase that ends on a dramatic headland with exposed rocks reaching out into the Hauraki Gulf. Bring a picnic and enjoy this historic site.

The impressive white building featured here was one of the country's five strategic locations for a communications network in the 1930s. During WWII it provided key contact with New Zealand forces stationed in the Pacific.

It was used for regional maritime and emergency radio services from the mid-1960s, before being decommissioned in 1993. Today, it houses an important archive of traditional radio equipment which is maintained and operated by amateur radio operators Musick Point Radio Group.

WHERE TO START?
Walk towards the radio building, then veer left to the headland, where you'll see a small pathway. Follow to the end, then clamber down the very steep steps leading to a rocky outcrop. Low tide will give you more options to explore at the bottom of the steps. If you're queasy with heights, perhaps loiter at the upper lookouts which still have excellent views.

MĀORI HISTORY
Te Naupata is the name for the entire peninsula, and it was the site of Te Waiarohia o Ngaitai Pā. The settlement's formidable headland position had strategic views over the Hauraki Gulf. Because of tribal warfare, it was abandoned in 1821 and is considered wāhi tapu/sacred. You can still see the deep defensive ditch through the north end of the Howick Golf Course.

NAMING
Musick Point was renamed in 1942 after American aviation pioneer Captain Edwin Musick, who piloted the first Pan American Airways flights from the United States to New Zealand in 1937.

IMPORTANT
There are dangerous cliffs and steep steps on the headland. The access road gate closes at 6pm. Beware of stray golf balls as you drive past the golf course.

EAST AUCKLAND

FIND OUT MORE
musickpointradio.org

BUCKLANDS BEACH
ŌHUIARANGI | PIGEON MOUNTAIN

Are the kids free range? This prominent peak, topped with gnarly pine trees, will make them adventurers.

This 55-metre-tall volcano was once nearly three times the size it is today. However, quarrying for roading material on the privately-owned northern side substantially destroyed the craters. Luckily, the southern side was set aside as a domain in the 1880s. Thousands of native shrubs and trees have been planted in recent years to encourage native kererū/wood pigeons back to this pretty maunga/mountain.

MĀORI HISTORY

Terracing around the perimeter of the volcano are the remnants of a Māori pā site. Artefacts were discovered by students in the 1960s and you might spy some shells exposed in the earth from domestic middens (rubbish heaps). Porokaiwhiri/pigeonwood covered the maunga before European settlement. Its juicy reddish-orange fruits attracted native kererū/wood pigeons, which the mountain is named after.

INFORMATION

GRADE: Easy/Hard

ACCESSIBILITY: Dirt paths and steep steps.

TIME: 1 hour (about 1 km) for a casual explore. More at low tide to clamber around the rocks.

LOCATION: Drive through Howick Golf Club off Musick Point Road, to the headland car park.

DOGS: On leads.

INFORMATION

GRADE: Medium

ACCESSIBILITY: Steep clamber up to the top and uneven surfaces.

TIME: 30 min for a quick explore.

LOCATION: Car park on Pigeon Mountain Road.

DOGS: On leads.

NATURE DISCOVERY

BY THE SEA

SHORELINE AND ROCK POOLS

Battered by the tides and blistering-hot summers, the creatures that call the shoreline and shallow rock pools home are some of the hardiest in New Zealand. Not only do they face the surging ocean every day but they also risk becoming a tasty morsel for passing birds when the tide retreats and their watery home becomes shallower and less able to protect them.

Rock pools are great spots to observe crabs, fish and snails, although you may need to patiently wait while they emerge from hiding under rocks and in crevices.

1. KĀUNGA | HERMIT CRABS

These hungry little scavengers make their homes in abandoned snail shells. They feed at night on algae and detritus (debris and dead matter) that floats down through the ocean. During the day they are often spotted in rock pools. When they grow, they 'moult' their shell to find a bigger shell to protect them. This often involves trading shells with other crabs, after they've both probed and rocked their potential homes to check for suitability. Hermit crabs are vulnerable to predators because of their thin shells.
Image © Kat Bolstad

2. NEPTUNE'S NECKLACE

This bubbly-looking seaweed is commonly found in rock pools at mid-tide levels throughout New Zealand and Australia. It's often brown, although can be orange or green in colour too. It feels slimy to touch and the slime helps it stay moist when exposed to air. The beads are filled with gas which allows them to rise to the surface and obtain sunlight, and water which keeps them hydrated. Also known as sea grapes or bubbleweed.

3. TIOTIO | BARNACLES

These intriguing critters start life as a shrimp-like creature that finds a spot to call home by cementing its head onto a rock. Over time, it builds a limestone structure that has a trapdoor on top that the barnacle can open and shut. It waves its hairy legs in the water to catch unsuspecting plankton floating by. If it's successful, it drags the plankton back into its shell before devouring it.

4. KAPU PARAHUA CUSHION STARFISH

These starfish are the most likely to be spotted along the coastline and in tidal rock pools. They can live for 10 years, and scavenge on living and dead organisms by extending their stomach outside of their body to cover and digest their prey. They usually have five arms and look as spongy as a soft cushion. They come in plenty of different colours: red, orange and pink through to bluish-green and black.

EAST AUCKLAND

BEACHLANDS
MOTUKARAKA | FLAT ISLAND

Visit at low tide to explore the uninhabited 'Island of the Karaka', tantalisingly perched at the end of a long, shallow shell bank.

INFORMATION

GRADE: Medium

ACCESSIBILITY: Sand, rocks and mud.

TIME: 1 hour 20 min (about 4 km) return.

FACILITIES: Sunkist Bay Reserve has a playground and toilets.

LOCATION: Sunkist Bay Reserve, Ealing Crescent, near Beachlands Wharf.

DOGS: No dogs allowed on the beach between 10am and 5pm during the summer.

Start at the western end of Sunkist Bay Reserve and walk over the exposed sand bar for about 500 metres to reach the island. Look out for the cockles hiding in the shallows and see if you can spot the shag colony around the back of the island. Locals affectionately call this low-profile island Flat Island. After Māori occupation, the island was at times farmed for potatoes — and rabbit breeding! — until a fire swept across the island for three days in 1965, burning everything to a crisp apart from a couple of hardy pōhutukawa trees. Kids will love to poke around in the caves as they channel their inner Robinson Crusoe.

MĀORI HISTORY

The former Ngāti Pāoa pā was home to several hundred Māori in the late 18th century. They cultivated traditional crops, including kūmara and rauaruhe/bracken fern, to supplement the abundant kaimoana/seafood available. Tragically, the island was invaded by another iwi seeking revenge who massacred nearly the entire community. Aside from short-lived European farming activity, the island has remained uninhabited. The site is considered wāhi tapu/sacred.

KARAKA TREE

Named after the Māori word for orange, the karaka tree is widespread in coastal habitats. The fruit ripens from mid-summer to autumn, and although the fruit flesh is edible, the fresh kernels are highly toxic. Karaka groves were common around pā sites because the fruit is nutritious.

WHEN TO VISIT

The island is accessible for approximately three hours either side of low tide. If you want to circumnavigate the island, make sure you start your adventure at least one hour before low tide. It gets muddy, so bring an old pair of sneakers.

85

EAST AUCKLAND

TOYOTA KIWI GUARDIANS
ŌMANA REGIONAL PARK

This activity trail meanders through a working farm park where you can play on a Māori-themed playground, listen out for the native pīwakawaka/fantail, say hello to the furry farm animals or just sit and relax on a grassy bank and soak up the stunning views over Waitematā Harbour. Bring your togs and take a dip at high tide.

This adventure is part of the Toyota Kiwi Guardians programme. Before you visit, download an activity sheet from kiwiguardians.co.nz or use the one in this book. Claim a medal when you find the unique code written on the Kiwi Guardian Post.

INFORMATION

GRADE: Easy

ACCESSIBILITY: Mixture of grass and gravel. Walking only.

TIME: 1 hour 15 min (2.5 km) for the loop.

FACILITIES: Toilets and playground.

LOCATION: Ōmana Beach Road, Maraetai.

DOGS: On leads within signposted areas.

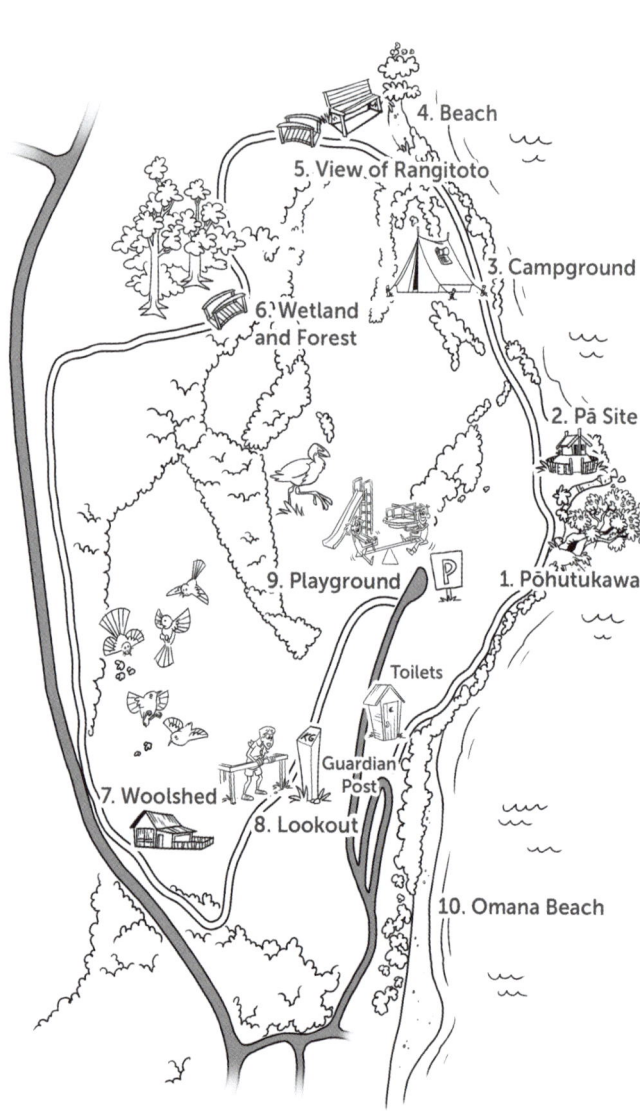

Map locations:
1. Pōhutukawa
2. Pā Site
3. Campground
4. Beach
5. View of Rangitoto
6. Wetland and Forest
7. Woolshed
8. Lookout
9. Playground
10. Omana Beach

86

EAST AUCKLAND

1. **NATURAL WONDERS:** I spy with my little eye a huge pōhutukawa tree. Can you find it?

2. **PĀ SITE:** Years ago, Māori lived around this ancient pā. Why do you think this was a good place for a pā?

3. **CAMPING GROUND:** Follow the footprints past the clifftop camping ground. Where would you set up camp?

4. **NATURE HUNT:** Arrrrrr. Arrrrrr. There's treasure hidden all over this beach. Can you find it?

5. **VIEW OF RANGITOTO ISLAND:** Look for the seat with magical views. Can you see Rangitoto Island from there?

6. **WETLAND AND FOREST:** Keep following the perimeter walk and make a list of how many creatures and birds you find sneaking through the forest.

7. **WOOLSHED:** This is where farmers round up the woolly sheep. Can you spot any?

8. **LOOKOUT:** Check out the amazing views of Tīkapa Moana/Hauraki Gulf! How many islands can you see from here?

9. **MĀORI-THEMED PLAYGROUND:** Learn about special stories, taonga/treasures and ngā manu/birds. Can you find out the traditional name of Tāmaki Strait?

10. **ŌMANA BEACH:** Home to all sorts of native birds like tōrea/variable oystercatcher and tarāpunga/red-billed seagulls. How many can you spot?

Image and content courtesy of Toyota Kiwi Guardians.

MARAETAI BEACH

MARAETAI COASTAL PATHWAY

Take in the highlights of the Pōhutukawa Coast and its postcard-worthy white-sand beaches. It's fun to explore by foot, or ideal for newly-minted riders zipping along on two wheels.

Maraetai Beach is a classic Kiwi summer spot with pōhutukawa trees and pristine beaches. It also has a plethora of ice-cream shops touting their wares. And if the crowds are too much, drive east along the coast until you find a secluded patch of sand. There are a couple of ways to maximise your visit. If you're feeling frisky, attack the 6-kilometre (one way) Beachlands-Maraetai Walkway which takes you past important archaeological and cultural sites. But if you're looking for a more kid-friendly adventure, the 4-kilometre (return) section between Maraetai Beach and Ōmana Regional Park still has plenty of highlights. This shorter route will take you through the rocky headlands of Te Pene Point and past small bays where you can jump off the bikes and take a cooling dip. Bring lunch to cook on the electric barbecues at Ōmana Beach.

INFORMATION

GRADE: Easiest

ACCESSIBILITY: Well-graded paths.

TIME: 2 hour (4 km return) to walk, picnic and swim.

FACILITIES: Playgrounds, toilets and cafés.

LOCATION: Plenty of parking near Maraetai Park. The path starts behind the Maraetai Beach Boating Club.

DOGS: Both on- and off-lead signposted areas.

87

EAST AUCKLAND

CLEVEDON
OLD THORP'S QUARRY WATERFALL

This small moss-draped waterfall cascades over the rim of a disused quarry into a regenerating wetland.

Little explorers will love this short, easy walk. A well-graded dirt track leads you to the boardwalk which passes through a small wetland area. Peek into the shallow stream beside the path to see if you can spot any critters.

The koru-shaped viewing platform has seating to perch on while you absorb the history of this former industrial site. Two ridgelines surround the quarry, and the freshwater wetland is currently being restored.

Historical photographs show the greywacke quarry's heydays during the early 1900s. The extracted rock helped build roads and footpaths within the region.

Native forest and swampland covered Clevedon before the 13th century. And despite periods of intensive logging and burning for pasture, the Clevedon Science Reserve has managed to retain valuable ecological stands of lowland and riparian broadleaf forest. Keep an eye out for taraire, pūriri, rimu and kahikatea.

INFORMATION

GRADE: Easiest

ACCESSIBILITY: Very shallow steps, board walk and dirt paths.

TIME: 15 min return.

FACILITIES: Toilets, picnic area and confidence course.

LOCATION: Thorps Quarry Road, Clevedon.

DOGS: On leads.

IMPORTANT

A kauri dieback station by the bridge prevents buggies using the pathway. Bring insect repellent for the active biters hanging around near the picnic table.

EAST AUCKLAND

CLEVEDON
TŌTARA WALKING TRACK

Known to locals as the 'stairway to heaven', this adventure involves climbing the side of a ridgeline to a lookout with 360-degree views including the bush-clad Coromandel Peninsula.

An impressive raised staircase near the start of this walk climbs steeply past a mature stand of kauri. While the wooden structure protects the native tree's roots from kauri dieback disease, it doesn't help the lungs! Feel the burn as you continue up multiple flights of stairs to the lookout. Be warned that Lycra-clad locals will probably breeze past you as you pause for a breather.

This 100-hectare patch of native bush overlooks the Wairoa River and is home to a noisy collection of native birds including the friendly pīwakawaka/fantail.

The views from the top are well worth the climb. Out east you can see the turquoise Hauraki Gulf and the Coromandel Peninsula, while off to the west on a good day you can spy the Waitākere Ranges.

You can make this into a loop track by continuing past the lookout then back down to the car park, which closes at 9pm in summer and 7pm in winter.

ACCESSIBILITY
Despite the stairs, this is a doable walk for little kids. Just take your time and be prepared for a few piggy-back rides if the going gets too challenging for your little explorer. Have plenty of bribes on hand!

INFORMATION

GRADE: Medium/Hard

ACCESSIBILITY: Dirt path, boardwalk and stairs.

TIME: Brisk 1 hour or 1 hour 30 min (about 3 km) with younger kids return.

FACILITIES: Toilets, picnic area and confidence course.

LOCATION: Thorps Quarry Road, Clevedon.

DOGS: On leads.

89

HŪNUA FALLS

EAST AUCKLAND

HŪNUA RANGES REGIONAL PARK
HŪNUA FALLS LOOP WALK

Join the crowds admiring this waterfall as it tumbles over a volcanic cliff into a pool 30 metres below, before climbing through forest to see the falls from another vantage point.

INFORMATION

GRADE: Easy

ACCESSIBILITY: Dirt path, boardwalk and steps.

TIME: 20 min (800 m) return. More for visiting the waterfall.

FACILITIES: Toilets, drinking fountain and picnic spots.

LOCATION: Plenty of parking at the end of Falls Road, Hūnua.

DOGS: No dogs allowed on the loop. On-lead elsewhere.

This waterfall is popular due to its easy accessibility — a mere minute's stroll from the car park. However, you may need to wait your turn to capture the classic 'catching a waterfall in your hands' shot that seems popular here with tourists. Bring a picnic and set up near the edge of the plunge pool and let the kids dip their toes in the water. It's buggy-friendly to the waterfall.

After you have admired the falls, clean your shoes of any dangerous kauri dieback spores at the cleaning station before crossing over the bridge. A pinhead-sized speck of soil containing the pathogen is enough to spread the disease, which is lethal to kauri.

The loop crosses a handful of boardwalks as it steadily climbs towards a lookout where you can see the bush-clad Hūnua Falls. This vantage point also gives you a bird's-eye view of the upper reaches of the waterfall.

The waterfall is on the Wairoa River, the headwaters of which nestle deep within the Hūnua Ranges. After its meandering journey, the river emerges into the Hauraki Gulf. It's the second-longest river in the Auckland region.

The river follows the route of the Wairoa Fault, which has uplifted basement greywacke rocks. These ancient rocks are the country's most common rock type, and were formed on the margins of the Gondwana super-continent between 300 and 100 million years ago. More recently, scientists suggest that magma (molten rock) rose through the fault and created a small basalt volcano here about 1.3 million years ago.

Complete the loop back to the car park. This walk is ideal for younger kids wanting a mini-adventure. The loop is only suitable for walking.

IMPORTANT
Swimming is not recommended at the waterfall as there are dangerous underwater ledges.

91

EAST AUCKLAND

HŪNUA RANGES REGIONAL PARK
COSSEYS GORGE TRACK

This trail leads you into a shallow gorge before climbing steadily to an impressive engineering feat nestled in 14,000 hectares of native forest.

INFORMATION

GRADE: Medium

ACCESSIBILITY: Dirt path, stream, road and steps.

TIME: 2 hour (about 6 km) return. More for picnics.

FACILITIES: Toilets at Hūnua Falls and Cosseys Dam.

LOCATION: Plenty of parking at the end of Falls Road, Hūnua.

DOGS: On leads but not near the dam.

From the car park, cross over the bridge and turn left at the junction. Shortly along the trail, the path dips down to Cosseys Creek, where there is a shallow stream crossing. There are plenty of boulders to hop across or just whip off your shoes and stroll through the water.

It's a steady climb beside the stream through a mixture of native bush and under a canopy of predominantly tawa trees near where the trail emerges by the dam. This vast forest filters about 2,300 millimetres of rain annually into four working dams located throughout the ranges.

Along the way, there are a few picturesque spots to sit beside the stream and listen out for one of the country's rarest birds, the kōkako. Cloaked in grey feathers with black patches across their eyes, they also have electric-blue wattles under their beaks. Kōkako were once common in this block of hilly country; however, now only about 250 birds remain. The Hūnua Kōkako Recovery Project wants to boost the population to 500 birds by 2025. The ranges are also a refuge for the native primitive pepeketua/Hochstetter's frog.

The trail ends at Cosseys Reservoir, which you can amble alongside, peer over the grass-clad Cosseys Dam, have a bite to eat and see if you can spot any water flowing into the reservoir's UFO-shaped drainage hole. You can either return to the main car park on the same trail or walk down Cossey Access Road for a little bit of variety, before connecting back with the track again. Look out for the wooden signpost on your left. There are plenty of stairs to jiggle the kneecaps on the way down.

COSSEYS DAM

In the wake of WWII, Auckland's booming population and industrial growth meant the city's demand for water outstripped what the existing Waitākere dams could supply. So when Cosseys Dam officially opened in 1955, with its 14 billion litres of water capacity,

EAST AUCKLAND

Aucklanders heaved a sigh of relief. Water from this earth-and-rock dam is gravity fed to the Ardmore Water Treatment Plant, then distributed to homes and businesses across the city.

The 42-metre-high dam is on the migratory paths of native fish and eels, so Watercare staff trap juvenile fish downstream and transfer them upstream past the dam between October and March. Because eels start to migrate to subtropical waters near Tonga in about April, staff also trap eels living in the dam and release them downstream.

EXTEND YOUR ADVENTURE

From the dam, you can continue on the Cossey/Massey Loop, which takes you back to the car park.

Allow three hours for the entire 8.3-kilometre loop from the Hūnua Falls Car Park. There are plenty of beautiful views, native forest and giant kauri trees along the way.

Top right image © Auckland Council

EAST AUCKLAND

HŪNUA RANGES REGIONAL PARK
HŪNUA SUSPENSION BRIDGE PATH

This pretty path is tucked away from the bustling Hūnua Falls and is well worth a visit with the kids. There's plenty of dense forest to stroll through, and a highlight is the view over Wairoa Reservoir.

Starting from the wooden suspension bridge over the Wairoa Stream, this walk climbs through native forest for about 20 minutes to the first lookout, before becoming more undulating to the next lookout. Luckily both have seats for a quick rest as you soak up the views and listen out for the chirping of friendly native birds. See if you can spot any pīwakawaka/fantails showing off with some aerial acrobatics.

Despite the steps, the path gradient is relatively steady, so it's easily doable if you take your time.

The path passes through a dramatic stand of spindly trees and lush ferns after the lookout, to another viewing spot above the reservoir, before dropping down to Wairoa Dam.

After admiring the bush-clad reservoir, you can follow the four-wheel-drive gravel road down past the picnic area and toilets, and back to the suspension bridge.

There's a small area for parking near the suspension bridge. You can walk from the bigger car park which you'll see as you drive in but it's a bit of a hike with little kids. Save their energy for the adventure!

DAM FACTS

The earth-and-rock dam was completed in 1975 and is 47 metres high. Its crest length is 213 metres. The lake covers 98 hectares when full, and its storage capacity is 11.6 gigalitres (1 gigalitre = 1 billion litres of water). The total catchment area of the dam is 1,300 hectares, and the average rainfall is 1,629 millimetres a year. Phew!

NATURE DISCOVERY

PEKAPEKA-TŌU-ROA
LONG-TAILED BAT

Auckland is home to these unique native mammals. However, habitat loss, feral cats and rats are reducing their population throughout the country.

They have been recorded in the Waitākere and Hūnua ranges, Riverhead, Pākiri and Swanson, and are capable of covering long distances between forest remnants to feed and roost.

The little bats weigh just 8 to 14 grams and have a wingspan of about 250 millimetres.

Long-tailed bats munch on flying insects like moths, mayflies and mosquitoes.

They are less active in winter and can even enter a semi-hibernation state to conserve energy during the chillier months of the year.

They roost upside down in small cavities in large old canopy trees (including dead trees) like rimu, pūriri, tōtara (left) and pukatea.

They are social animals and spend time feeding and roosting with colonies of 10 to 50 other bats.

Breeding females give birth to one pup each year, and these hang onto mum during feeding flights until they reach adolescence at around four to six weeks.

Bat image © Gerard Kelly

INFORMATION

GRADE: Medium

ACCESSIBILITY: Gravel, road, dirt paths and steps.

TIME: 1 hour and 30 min (about 4 km) for the loop.

FACILITIES: Picnic tables and toilets available below the dam.

LOCATION: Otau Road off Moumoukai Road, Hūnua.

DOGS: On leads.

EAST AUCKLAND

KAWAKAWA BAY | FIRTH OF THAMES
TAWHITOKINO BEACH PATH

This secluded patch of paradise is only accessible by foot, which stops the masses from spoiling the serenity, and earns it the title of one of the city's 'secret beaches'.

INFORMATION

GRADE: Medium

ACCESSIBILITY: Sand, rocks, steps and well-graded path.

TIME: 60 min (2 km) return.

FACILITIES: Toilet beside car park, and at the far end of Tawhitokino Beach.

LOCATION: The end of Kawakawa Bay Coast Road. The road narrows significantly after Kawakawa Bay.

DOGS: On leads.

Starting from Waiti Bay, this coastal walk skirts around a rocky headland streaked with multi-coloured rocks and covered in oyster shells. Jandals and bare feet don't stand a chance here – bring shoes to save delicate toes.

After navigating the headland and admiring the massive pōhutukawa roots dangling over the cliff, walk across the sheltered Tūtūrau Bay – it's hard to resist taking a dip in its aquamarine waters – to the signposted trail leading you across Papanui Point.

There's plenty of stairs up, but the rewards of seeing islands dotted in the sparkling waters of the Hauraki Gulf coastline take the edge off the short, thigh-burning climb.

Descending from the headland, the picturesque 1.4-kilometre-long Tawhitokino Beach appears. At the base of the stairs, budding geologists can peer at the sloped, exposed bedrock to see regionally significant outcrops of deformed chert beds which could date from the Triassic age (about 200 to 250 million years ago).

For shorter adventures, hang about near the stairs, or with more time, stroll along the white sandy beach to the campsite.

Pōhutukawa trees provide pockets of shade beside the cliff, perfect for picnics and keeping cool mid-summer. This is an excellent swimming beach.

LOW TIDE ACCESS

Ensure you complete the walk within two hours either side of low tide. Check the tides before you go to allow adequate time.

Top image © Gary Clare

EAST AUCKLAND

TOETOE

These giant grasses are an iconic part of the landscape, with large light golden-yellow flower plumes draping off tall stems.

But toetoe are often confused with the invasive pampas weed (right).

The easiest way to distinguish between the two is by looking at the flower head; pampas have dense, fluffy flower heads like a feather duster, while toetoe (below) have drooping flower heads. The general rule of thumb is that toetoe flowers before Christmas, while pampas flowers afterwards.

Pampas also has the unfortunate nickname of cutty grass – something off-piste adventurers try to avoid!

97

EAST AUCKLAND

WAIHIHI BAY | FIRTH OF THAMES
WAHARAU BUSH PATH

This short adventure offers easy strolling through native forest with plenty of bird-life to listen out for at Waharau Regional Park, on the eastern slopes of the Hūnua Ranges.

Stretching to the gravelly shores of Waihihi Bay on Tīkapa Moana-o-Hauraki/Firth of Thames, this regional park covers the gamut of varying landscapes: farmland, river banks to native forest.

The shortest adventure on offer is this well-graded bush path that follows a forest stream before slowly ascending past tānekaha/celery pine, kauri and horoeka/lancewood. Spindly mānuka arch over the fern edged trail, while moss-draped rimu trees glow with dappled sunlight.

Listen out for kererū crashing through the canopy, or pause to spot any pīwakawaka/fantails trailing behind. Also calling these ranges home are tūī, ruru/morepork, miromiro/tomtit and kākā. In the stream, you might spy kōura/freshwater crayfish.

Plant labels identify a dozen or so native species that thrive here, including mamaku and silver ferns.

INFORMATION

GRADE: Easy

ACCESSIBILITY: Well-graded tracks and steps.

TIME: 45 min (about 2 km) for an easy stroll of the loop.

FACILITIES: Toilets at the information shelter.

LOCATION: Waharau Regional Park, East Coast Road, Waihihi Bay.

DOGS: On leads.

STARTING POINT
Drive past the visitor centre and you'll see the trailhead shortly ahead on your right, opposite a small car park.

EXTEND YOUR ADVENTURE
The 11-kilometre-long Waharau Ridge Track will take about 3.5 hours to complete and leads to panoramic views of the Coromandel Peninsula. Download a trail map from the Auckland Council website.

NATURE DISCOVERY

KUAKA
BAR-TAILED GODWIT

These amazing birds make the most epic non-stop flights of any non-seabirds. Because they don't dive for food, they fly for up to nine days on an empty tummy.

The godwits begin arriving at the Firth of Thames from early September after travelling for more than 12,000 kilometres from the Arctic regions of Alaska and Siberia. They are one of 35 species to arrive in New Zealand each summer to either fatten up on the plentiful food here or to avoid their chilly frozen homes.

FIND OUT MORE
shorebirds.org.nz

Some 80,000 godwits arrive each year and can also be seen in various spots around the country including the Mānukau Harbour, Farewell Spit and the Avon Heathcote estuary. They spend the warmer months here before heading north again.

Visit Miranda in autumn when the godwits leave in small flocks. A number of birds have been recaptured more than 18 years since they were banded — now that's a lot of air miles!

MĀORI NAME
Māori named the godwits kuaka. Because of their migratory habits, they were a bird of mystery. "Kua kite te kōhanga kuaka? Who has seen the nest of the kuaka?"

KŌURA | CRAYFISH

Camouflaged with mottled dark green shell-like skin, freshwater crayfish shelter among stones or burrow into muddy stream beds. During the day, only the occasional black beady eye or waving feeler can be spotted, as it's mostly at night when these scavengers emerge to feed on old leaves and small insects floating by. They don't hunt; they like food to be delivered!

Four pairs of legs allow them to move quickly, so be careful as their pincers can give a painful nip if threatened.

Two species live in New Zealand: the North Island species (about 70 mm long), and the east and south of the South Island species (about 80 mm long).

KAREKARE BEACH

WEST COAST

DISCOVER
WEST COAST ADVENTURES

Ditch the city and head west towards the Tasman Sea to get some hot black sand between your toes. Clamber through sea caves that once hosted rollicking dances, or dip your toes in palm-shrouded pools.

HIGHLIGHTS

CLAMBER UP AND DOWN ANCIENT SAND DUNES AT LAKE WAINAMU.

Walk along a shallow stream towards vast black-sand dunes, before diving into a dune lake for an afternoon of floating around (p113).

WATCH THE TASMAN SEA CRASH AGAINST SEA CLIFFS ON THE TASMAN LOOKOUT PATH.

From this headland, you get a bird's-eye view of Piha's Lion Rock but also get to explore The Gap, where the ocean erupts into explosive foam between cliffs (p122).

VISIT IN SUMMER TO SEE HUNDREDS OF NOISY TAKAPŪ/ AUSTRALASIAN GANNETS NESTING NEAR THE MAUKATIA GANNET PATH.

Wild winds and scorching-hot summers batter this rugged headland, yet hundreds of gannets return to nest here each year from Australia. It's an impressive sight (p104).

WEST COAST
MURIWAI BEACH

This wild beach stretches 50 kilometres north to the Kaipara Harbour, while its rugged southern cliffs are home to an impressive gannet colony – and a few bellowing blow-holes!

Despite being well-known for its colony of takapū/Australasian gannets, this small coastal settlement has loads of kid-friendly activities to make a memorable outing. The expansive beach will tucker out the most active explorers in your tribe, and if the tide is right, you may see the blow-holes on the rock shelf in action. Even if the gannet colony isn't a drawcard for the family, the various lookouts on Ōtakamiro Point are worth exploring for their impressive views of the wild Tasman Sea.

HISTORY

Various iwi occupied this food-rich valley since the earliest period of human settlement in the area – including small groups of Māori from outside the area who were later involved in gum-digging. The land surrounding the pā/fortified village site on Ōtakamiro Point had fertile soil where kūmara was grown, and the nearby forest was a resource providing a wide variety of medicinal plants, foods and building materials.

MOTOR RACING

In the early 1920s, the beach held New Zealand's first 25-mile (40-kilometre) motor race. Howard Nattrass won the inaugural race in a time of 17 minutes in a stripped V8 Cadillac.

MĀORI NAME

Muriwai means 'backwater or lagoon'. The beach was originally considered part of a more extensive section of coastline called Te One Rangatira, meaning 'the chiefly beach', which stretched from the Kaipara Harbour to Tokaraerae, 40 kilometres to the south.

HAVE YOU SEEN AN
ENDANGERED MĀUI DOLPHIN?

FIND OUT MORE
doc.govt.nz

Māui are the world's rarest and smallest dolphins and are on the edge of extinction. Only between 48 and 64 dolphins over one year of age are known to exist.

They live on the west coast of the north island from Maunganui Bluff to Whanganui, and you're most likely to spot them between the Manukau Harbour and Port Waikato. They were once common along the entire west coast of the North Island.

They look the same as Hector's dolphins but are genetically different. Māui used to be known as the North Island Hector's dolphin but in 2002 were classified as a separate subspecies. They both have a rounded black dorsal fin; all other dolphins have a sickle-shaped fin.

MĀUI DOLPHIN FIN

COMMON DOLPHIN FIN

These amazing dolphins are slow to reproduce, with females producing only one calf every two to four years.

Keep an eye out for Māui while you explore the coastline, as they are often spotted in water less than 20 metres deep. They have distinctive grey, white and black markings and a short snout. The males are slightly smaller and lighter than the females, which can grow to 1.7 metres in length and weigh up to 50 kilograms.

SPOTTED A MĀUI DOLPHIN?
Report any Māui dolphin sightings to the Department of Conservation by calling 0800 362 468. If possible, include location, GPS coordinates, number seen, time and date.

INFORMATION

GRADE: Easy

ACCESSIBILITY: Lots of hot black sand. Bring shoes.

TIME: Allow a few hours to explore the beach and have a picnic.

FOOD OUTLETS: Café.

RUBBISH: Bins provided.

GETTING THERE: Drive north on SH16 to Waimauku and turn left onto Muriwai Road. Follow to the end.

DOGS: Off-lead north of the surf tower but prohibited at all times south of the tower.

FACILITIES: Toilets by the car park.

IMPORTANT: Don't forget your sunscreen and hat!

THIS BEACH HAS STRONG RIPS, CURRENTS AND LARGE WAVES. LIFEGUARDS PATROL THE BEACH ONLY WHEN THE YELLOW AND RED FLAGS ARE DISPLAYED. ALWAYS SWIM BETWEEN THE FLAGS.

WEST COAST

MURIWAI
MAUKATIA GANNET PATH

Explore a headland battered by wild winds and scorching-hot summers that is home to thousands of takapū/Australasian gannets which return from Australia to nest here each year.

INFORMATION

GRADE: Easy/Medium

ACCESSIBILITY: Well-graded dirt and concrete paths, and steps.

TIME: 45 min (1.3 km) return to visit all the lookouts and complete the loop, or a short 15-min return stroll to the first lookout.

LOCATION: South end of Muriwai Beach.

DOGS: No dogs allowed.

This walk is one of Muriwai Regional Park's 'must-do' attractions, particularly in spring and summer when the gannet colony is clamouring with activity. It's well worth a trip to the park just for this unique experience.

From the southern end of Muriwai Beach, walk over the rock shelf to the small wooden staircase. If the conditions are right, you might see the little blow-hole happily bellowing away. The small lookout nearby is a safe spot from where you can watch all the action.

The wide path climbs up to the first lookout on Ōtakamiro Point where you can see the rock stack of Motutara Island. The viewing platform gets you very close to the occasionally pungent action as the gannets settle in for a summer of raising their chicks. Remarkably, the birds remain oblivious to the swarms of tourists who are taking selfies mere metres away.

Continue along the path to another lookout where you can see all the nests perched – sometimes seemingly precariously – on the steep rocky cliffs. In the 1900s the gannets nested on Oaia Island – the small, rounded island you can see just offshore – before moving to Motutara Island. The colony then outgrew their new home in the 1970s and encroached on the headland at Ōtakamiro.

From here you can either return to the beach or continue to the car park overlooking Maukatia/Māori Bay.

From the car park follow the signs for the Māori/Maukatia Bay track along the road, then the trail veers left into a patch of coastal forest

NATURE DISCOVERY

TĀKAPU
AUSTRALIAN GANNET

The ragged Ōtakamiro Point and rock stack of Motutara Island are home to about 1,200 pairs of takapū/Australasian gannets that return from Australia to breed each year.

From July the males start arriving, and busy themselves making and defending nests before their mates join them.

You'll see their mating rituals in early spring, and during the laying season from August, females will produce a single egg. But if the first egg is lost, they can lay a replacement egg within four weeks.

In about November, the breeding population reaches its peak, and during summer the colony is busy feeding their chicks before preparing to depart back to Australia between May and July.

These coastal seabirds have an impressive 1.8-metre wingspan, and you can feel the whoosh from their wings when they dive close to the viewing platforms.

Listen out for their distinctive 'urrah-urrah ' as they come into land or the 'oo-ah' which indicates their take-off is imminent. They often point to the sky with their bills, which can mean they're about to take flight. Look out for their bill-touching and bowing with their mate as they sweetly greet each other back at the nest.

INBUILT AIRBAGS
Gannets protect themselves during their torpedo-like ocean plunges with structures similar to a car's airbags in their body. While fishing, they can hit the water at speeds of up to 85 kilometres per hour from 40 metres above, to reach depths of about 11 metres. Ouch!

---

which is also a nesting ground for the ōi/grey-faced petrel. You'll come out near the playground and main car park where you started.

IMPORTANT
Take care on the rock shelf as it can become slippery from the ocean spray. Keep an eye on the kids around the exposed cliffs.

PARKING
If you're struggling to find a car park in the frenzy of mid-summer crowds, drive around to Maukatia/Māori Bay and walk the path in reverse.

EXTEND YOUR ADVENTURE
If you have time, drop down into the secluded Maukatia/Māori Bay (p107) to see some of the rock formations created from a submarine eruption 17 million years ago.

WEST COAST

MURIWAI
MITCHELSON LOOKOUT

This short stroll leads to a lookout with views along the vast black-sand beach out to Oaia Island and north for miles.

You can start the walk from almost opposite the café but if you're feeling a little lazy, you can drive to where it connects with Domain Crescent. There's less parking here, though — only room for a couple of cars.

From Domain Crescent there are plenty of towering nīkau palms and pōhutukawa trees lining the trail. You'll need to duck under a low pōhutukawa branch that has arched itself across the path.

At the lookout, there's a seat from where you can spy all the places you have visited in the coastal township, and marvel at how long the beach is. It's quite impressive.

A patchy coastal forest blankets the surrounding hillside with a few homes poking through, surrounded by a splash of green grass.

If you're tackling the 'big' option from Motutara Road near the café, you'll take the steps to Domain Crescent, where you'll pick the track up again 100 metres further up the road.

INFORMATION

GRADE: Easy

ACCESSIBILITY: Well-graded dirt path, steps and road.

TIME: 15 min return from Domain Crescent, or 30 min return (1 km) from Motukara Road.

LOCATION: Main car park at Muriwai Beach, or Domain Crescent.

DOGS: On leads.

OAIA ISLAND

This mounded island less than 2 kilometres offshore was the original nesting site for takapū/Australasian gannets but a population spike meant they outgrew the island and spread to nearby Motutara Island and Ōtakamiro Point.

Gannets still breed on the island, while kekeno/New Zealand fur seals and kororā/little penguins feed and rest here.

New Zealand artist Colin McCahon referred to the island as 'Moby Dick Island'.

WEST COAST

MURIWAI
MAUKATIA | MĀORI BAY

This sheltered bay provides some respite from the crowds at Muriwai Beach and has some intriguing geological formations to interest budding geologists.

From the car park, take the gravel path down to the beach. Short on time? Just head to the base of Ōtakamiro Point where a blow-hole often sprays foam out onto the beach.

The blow-hole and nearby sea caves were formed by waves that over time slowly inched their way into rock fractures. A collapsed sea cave separated Motutara Island from the mainland. The rock stack is now perched alone in the pounding surf.

Further down the beach, peer up at the cliffs and the dramatic pillow lava formations. You'll easily spy the two circular shapes that were once large feeder tubes carrying andesitic basaltic lava across an ancient seabed from the Waitākere Volcano which was erupting as 'recently' as 17 million years ago. The cliff face and tubes became visible after enormous forces pushed the volcano up, followed by erosion from the ocean.

Keep walking towards the southern end of the beach where there are rock pools to spot little ocean-dwelling critters; here's a good opportunity to practise your sea slug and sea lettuce identification skills.

IMPORTANT
Take care around the sea caves. If you're exploring past the southern tip of the beach, you'll need to be careful of the incoming tide. No dogs are allowed because the beach is home to kororā/little penguins (p111).

INFORMATION

GRADE: Easy

ACCESSIBILITY: Steep gravel path to beach.

TIME: 15 min return to the blow-hole, or 30 min return to the rock formations further south along the beach.

LOCATION: The car park is off Waitea Road.

DOGS: No dogs allowed.

107

WEST COAST
TE HENGA | BETHELLS BEACH

Explore this peaceful black-sand beach with its sea cave, or the ancient dunes nearby that hide a vast dune lake, perfect for diving into during the hotter months.

This beach is where the Waitākere River finally emerges into the Tasman Sea after its journey from deep within the Waitākere Ranges. Historically, the river was an important transport hub for Māori waka. However, damming upstream in the 1920s substantially subdued its flow. Today, it makes a fun lagoon, and at low tide, it's a great safe spot for littlies to splash around. The main beach stretches south to a headland and sea caves which are illuminated by glow-worms at night.

Human settlement in this valley stretches back more than 1,000 years. Significant sites dotted around this beach include pā/fortified village remnants and walkways. It wasn't until the mid-1800s when Europeans arrived that the landscape changed significantly due to logging and farming. This coastal settlement has become a destination for surfers, both on waves and sand dunes, and plenty of tourists keen to soak up the relaxed beach vibes.

FILMING LOCATIONS
The beach has appeared in plenty of music videos, movies and television shows, including Shania Twain ('Forever and for Always') and Taylor Swift ('Out of the Woods'), *Crouching Tiger Hidden Dragon: Sword of Destiny* and local favourites *Xena: Warrior Princess* and *Hercules: The Legendary Journeys*.

MĀORI NAME
Te Henga means 'sand' and refers to the long dunes beside the beach.

TE HENGA WALKWAY
This clifftop walk connects Te Henga to just south of Muriwai and offers incredible views of the wild west coast. The 10-kilometre walk from Bethells Road to Constable Road takes approximately 3.5 hours one way. However, you can shorten it to 40 minutes one way if you just walk from Bethells Road to O'Neills Bay.

WEST COAST

LAKE WAINAMU
TE HENGA WETLAND

Te Henga is the largest remaining wetland in Auckland – near Lake Wainamu, tucked behind the dunes of Bethells Beach.

Its sprawling 140 hectares is teeming with more than 300 recorded species of plant life, 45 bird species and 6 species of native fish.

Volunteers are transforming this landscape by trapping pest animals and removing invasive plants. Restorative native planting is also helping to attract the secretive matuku-hūrepo/Australasian bittern, pūweto/spotless crake and mātātā/fernbird, which are returning to roost in the wetland.

The endangered pāteke/brown teal (right) was released into the wetland in 2015 after substantial pest eradication to make their new home safer. Previously these small brown ducks used to be found throughout the area and across more than 80 per cent of New Zealand, but predation by introduced mammals drastically reduced their population. Now, they are flourishing in the wetland and have started breeding.

MORE INFORMATION

To learn more about Habitat Te Henga, and how to lend a hand, visit the Forest and Bird website. Wetland image © Paul Hafner

INFORMATION

GRADE: Easy

ACCESSIBILITY: Lots of hot black sand. Bring shoes.

TIME: Allow a couple of hours to explore the beach, play in the shallow river and visit the cave.

FOOD OUTLETS: A pop-up food cart often operates near the car park.

RUBBISH: Bins provided.

GETTING THERE: Head northwest through Henderson and Swanson. Follow the signs.

DOGS: On leads.

FACILITIES: There are public toilets, outdoor showers and changing sheds near the car park.

IMPORTANT: Don't forget your sunscreen and hat!

THIS BEACH HAS STRONG RIPS AND CURRENTS AND LARGE WAVES. LIFEGUARDS PATROL THIS BEACH ONLY WHEN THE YELLOW AND RED FLAGS ARE DISPLAYED. SWIM BETWEEN THE FLAGS.

WEST COAST

TOYOTA KIWI GUARDIANS
TE HENGA | BETHELLS BEACH

Discover the rugged beauty and rich history of Auckland's west coast. This walk takes you through native bush, past clifftops with amazing views and down to a beautiful secluded West Coast beach.

Map locations:
1. Waitākere River
2. Bird Spotting
3. View Over Te Henga
4. Te Tai-o-Rehua / Tasman Sea
5. Native Bush
6. View Over O'Neill Bay
7. Trapping Boxes
8. O'Neill Bay
9. Pā Site
10. Coastal History
- Guardian Post

This adventure is part of the Toyota Kiwi Guardians programme. Before you visit, download an activity sheet from kiwiguardians.co.nz or use the one in this book. Claim a medal when you find the unique code written on the Kiwi Guardian Post.

1. WAITĀKERE RIVER: Imagine back when Māori iwi/tribes would travel up and down this river by waka/canoe. Can you see any creatures hiding in the water?

2. BIRD SPOTTING: Look at the bush next to you. Can you spot any birds playing in the trees?

3. VIEWS OVER TE HENGA: Look at that fantastic view! Did you know Te Henga means 'sand'? These dunes have been building up for over 4,000 years – that's sooooo long ago!

4. TE TAI-O-REHUA / TASMAN SEA: Did you know half of the world's marine species visit New Zealand's oceans? Keep your eye out for the critically endangered Māui dolphin that sometimes visits this stretch of coastline.

5. NATIVE BUSH: Can you find the loudest-singing bird in the bush? Tweet tweet.

6. VIEW OVER O'NEILL BAY: Congratulations, you made it to the top! Now stop, relax for a few minutes and take in that amazing view.

7. TRAPPING BOXES: These boxes help our native birds stay safe from predators. Do you know the names of any predators?

8. O'NEILL BAY: Time to explore! See how many interesting things you can collect on the shore. If you spot some rubbish, take it back to the bins in the car park.

9. PĀ SITE: Look over there, that's Kauwahaia Island, an old pā. Who do you think used to live there?

10. COASTAL HISTORY: Did you know that early Māori were expert ocean navigators? Many Māori lived in coastal areas like here because of the delicious kaimoana/seafood. What do you think they caught?

Image and content courtesy of Toyota Kiwi Guardians.

NATURE DISCOVERY

KORORĀ
LITTLE PENGUIN

Auckland's west coast is home to the world's smallest penguins, that come ashore under cover of darkness.

The penguins are primarily nocturnal on land, as they spend their days feeding at sea by themselves or in small groups of rarely more than six penguins. Before they return to their nesting areas at dusk, they congregate in small 'rafts' offshore to arrive home together. They are brilliant pursuit hunters in shallow waters and live up to their scientific name 'Eudyptula', which means 'good little diver'. They hunt for small fish, squid and krill within 15 to 20 kilometres of the coast.

These small birds stand at just over 25 centimetres tall and weigh about 1 kilogram. Their conservation status is 'at risk', with many colonies in decline due to introduced predators including cats, dogs and ferrets. They were once widely distributed along New Zealand coastlines but now seek offshore islands where there are fewer disturbances from predators and human activity.

Traditionally the penguins nested in underground burrows, under vegetation or between rocks and caves. But as the country's coastlines became more populated, they are often spotted nesting close to human settlements, under and around homes and boat sheds. Their noisy vocal displays can keep owners awake at night!

HOW TO KEEP KORORĀ SAFE:

Leave all penguins alone. Usually, scruffy birds are merely moulting. Put dogs on a lead around penguin areas and keep them away from nests. Warn others of nest locations.

TOYOTA KIWI GUARDIANS

CAN YOU SPY MĀUI DOLPHINS PLAYING CLOSE TO THE SHORE?

INFORMATION

GRADE: Medium

ACCESSIBILITY: Some steep and moderately tricky parts. Take care around coastal cliffs, slippery tracks and unpredictable waves or tides. Check weather and tide forecast before starting.

TIME: Allow 1 hour 30 min (about 4 km) return.

LOCATION: Parking just after the bridge before Bethells Beach.

DOGS: No dogs allowed.

NATURE DISCOVERY

RELAX AND LOOK UP
WHAT CLOUD IS THAT?

Clouds are made up of tiny water droplets and ice crystals, which are super small and can float in the air. When the droplets get large enough, you can see them as cloud or fog. If they become even larger, they can turn into rain or snow.

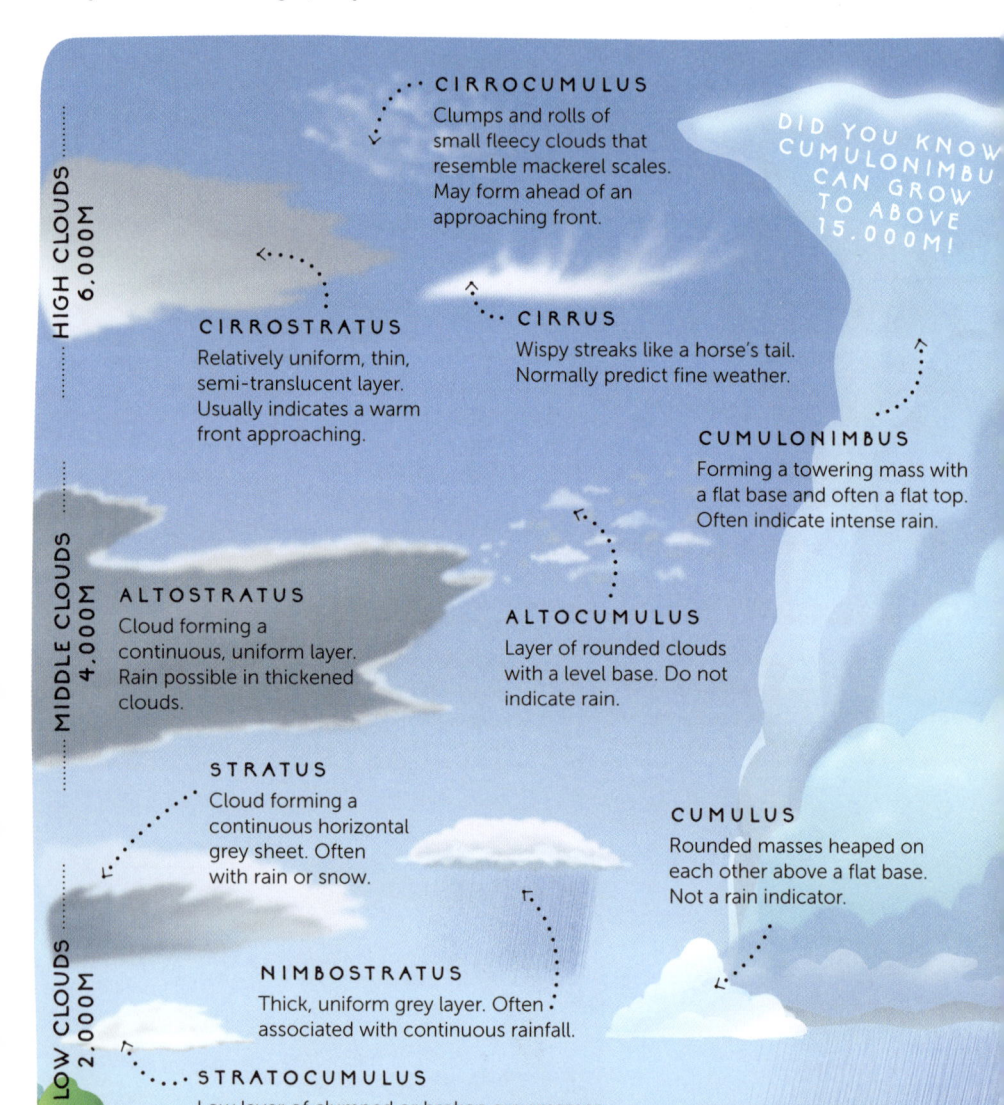

HIGH CLOUDS 6,000M

CIRROCUMULUS
Clumps and rolls of small fleecy clouds that resemble mackerel scales. May form ahead of an approaching front.

DID YOU KNOW CUMULONIMBUS CAN GROW TO ABOVE 15,000M!

CIRROSTRATUS
Relatively uniform, thin, semi-translucent layer. Usually indicates a warm front approaching.

CIRRUS
Wispy streaks like a horse's tail. Normally predict fine weather.

CUMULONIMBUS
Forming a towering mass with a flat base and often a flat top. Often indicate intense rain.

MIDDLE CLOUDS 4,000M

ALTOSTRATUS
Cloud forming a continuous, uniform layer. Rain possible in thickened clouds.

ALTOCUMULUS
Layer of rounded clouds with a level base. Do not indicate rain.

STRATUS
Cloud forming a continuous horizontal grey sheet. Often with rain or snow.

CUMULUS
Rounded masses heaped on each other above a flat base. Not a rain indicator.

LOW CLOUDS 2,000M

NIMBOSTRATUS
Thick, uniform grey layer. Often associated with continuous rainfall.

STRATOCUMULUS
Low layer of clumped or broken grey masses. Often seen before or after bad weather.

WEST COAST

TE HENGA | BETHELLS BEACH
LAKE WAINAMU

Ancient black dunes that have taken thousands of years to form are the perfect launching pad for kids to tear down before diving into a dune lake to cool off. This lake is an excellent summer wallowing hole for families.

INFORMATION

GRADE: Easy/Medium

ACCESSIBILITY: Shallow stream to walk through. Optional steep dunes to climb.

TIME: 45 min to 1 hour (about 4.5 km) return along the stream. More for swimming.

LOCATION: Well-signposted car park just after the bridge before Bethells Beach.

DOGS: No dogs allowed.

Bring your togs and inflatable animals for this outing. From the car park, follow the signs to the shallow stream which you can wade through towards the dunes looming in front of you. Follow the stream to the left and continue walking until you reach the lake.

Perch yourself on the lake's edge and soak up the atmosphere of this natural wonder. The rim can be steep, so if you have little kids, they may prefer to paddle by the stream entrance. Otherwise, let the older kids loose on the dunes – where they can tear down and jump straight into the fresh water.

Be prepared for burning HOT black sand. Bring shoes for the dunes as jandals offer zero protection for tootsies in deep sand. Also remember to slip, slop, slap and wrap as there's no shade by the lake.

EXTEND YOUR ADVENTURE

An additional 1-hour-long Lake Waimanu Loop Track continues around the lake to a picturesque waterfall. Look for the sign post on your left as you arrive near the dune lake. It can be boggy at times.

TOILET

There's a basic toilet signposted halfway to the lake but you'll need to climb up over a big dune. Best use the facilities at Bethells Beach before heading off on this adventure.

113

PIHA BEACH

WEST COAST

WEST COAST
PIHA BEACH

This laid-back coastal community has long been a drawcard for tourists wanting to escape and relax at this idyllic holiday spot sandwiched between the Waitākere Ranges and the mighty Tasman Sea.

This small settlement is home to about 600 residents year-round but this swells considerably on the weekend and during summer, when hundreds descend on the beach. Surfers and tourists have been making the pilgrimage to Piha since the 1930s. They were a keen bunch back then, considering the only way to get there was on a rough, pothole-riddled horse track. The road has been fully sealed only since 1983. Piha remains a popular spot for surfers to tackle the waves near Taitomo Island, near the southern end of the beach and by Lion Rock.

PIHA RESCUE
This beach was the setting for the succinctly named *Piha Rescue* television series, which showcased members of the Piha Surf Life Saving Club as they patrolled the beach. The reality show ran for more than 14 years.

INFORMATION

GRADE: Easy

ACCESSIBILITY: Lots of hot black sand! So, bring shoes for all the family.

TIME: Allow a couple of hours to explore the beach, grab a coffee and watch the kids paddle in the shallows.

FOOD OUTLETS: A couple of options.

RUBBISH: Bins provided.

GETTING THERE: From Titirangi Village take Scenic Drive and follow the signs to Piha. Plenty of parking at the main car park to the left.

DOGS: Dogs are prohibited south of Lion Rock. Follow the signs regarding dogs on North Piha Beach.

FACILITIES: There are public toilets and changing sheds in the middle of the beach.

IMPORTANT: Don't forget your sunscreen and hat!

THIS BEACH HAS STRONG RIPS AND CURRENTS, LARGE WAVES AND DEEP HOLES. LIFEGUARDS PATROL THE BEACH ONLY WHEN THE YELLOW AND RED FLAGS ARE DISPLAYED. ALWAYS SWIM BETWEEN THE FLAGS.

WEST COAST

NORTH PIHA
TE WAHA POINT

It's a steady climb to the lookout but while you catch your breath at the top, you can soak up the views down to the picturesque White's Beach, which is a hidden gem.

Stroll north along the beach from the North Piha car park towards the headland at Kohunui Bay. Keep an eye out for the walk's entrance near the base of one of the wooden poles – it's well hidden under overhanging pōhutukawa. Follow the sign that says Laid Thomson Track.

The path immediately climbs away from the beach, and you become sandwiched between a sheer rock face and wind-blown mounds of black sand. There are plenty of steps beneath the coastal forest, which has been weathered by brutal West Coast storms and caused the pōhutukawa trees to bend over the pathway, helpfully providing shelter from the summer sun.

Listen out for the roar of the ocean as you stroll along. Between small gaps in the forest, you can spot the prominent outcrop of Lion Rock which divides Piha Beach.

As you continue to climb, you can see why this headland was the site of Te Wahangū pā – one of a handful of historic Piha sites –

INFORMATION

GRADE: Medium

ACCESSIBILITY: Steps and dirt paths.

TIME: 1 hour return.

FACILITIES: Toilets halfway along North Piha Road.

LOCATION: Car park at the end of North Piha Road.

DOGS: No dogs allowed.

OĪ | GREY-FACED PETRELS

The headland is home to ōi/grey-faced petrels, which nest in the ground around the roots of pōhutukawa.

Only a handful of burrowing petrels still survives on the mainland, which makes this colony special.

They are an oceanic seabird and are impressive to watch soaring powerfully on long, narrow wings.

They have dark black-brown bodies, and at the base of the throat there is either grey or white contrast.

WEST COAST

due to its excellent vantage point surrounded by sheer cliffs.

At the track junction, follow the lookout track sign which leads to two seating spots overlooking White's Beach (above). See if you can spot any keen surfers tackling the waves at this small beach when the conditions are right. Return the same way you came. If you have time, there are some small cliff caves to explore but take care as there could be unstable rocks above.

ROCK CAIRN

The rock cairn at the lookout marks the descendants of the Rose and Laid Thomson family who gave land on both sides of the headland in the 1960s to the regional park to provide access for walkers to explore the area.

IMPORTANT

Take care with kids as there are steep drop-offs beside the path, particularly on the last section to the lookout, which is surrounded by up to 100-metre-high cliffs. Dogs are strictly prohibited on this walk because Kohunui Bay is home to plenty of native birds including kororā/little blue penguins and tōrea/variable oystercatchers.

117

WEST COAST

NORTH PIHA
MARAWHARA WALK

Ahhhh . . . escape the blistering sun as you stroll through a coastal forest to a stream with dappled sunlight poking through overhanging pōhutukawa trees.

INFORMATION

GRADE: Easiest

ACCESSIBILITY: Well-graded dirt path.

TIME: 30 min return. More for paddling.

FACILITIES: Toilets halfway along North Piha Road.

LOCATION: Parking is on North Piha Road by Marawhara Stream Bridge.

DOGS: On leads.

The trail leads inwards through a dense nīkau palm forest as it follows alongside the meandering Marawhara Stream which is slowly making its way to the ocean.

It's not a long walk, so you'll quickly arrive at the grassy glade. Keep walking, and you'll spy steps down to the stream a little further ahead.

This wide, shallow stream is ideal for kids to spend some time paddling or making rock cairns. It's a particularly idyllic spot with the diluted sunlight filtering through the surrounding trees arching over the swimming-hole.

On the return trip, look out for the thriving kawakawa bushes which have enormous leaves. And they must be tasty, considering how many hungry critters have been munching on them.

ACCESSIBILITY
This path is suitable for buggies but you'll need to navigate the small kauri dieback station near the track entrance and clean their wheels.

BLACK SANDS

The black sands on the west coast beaches are rich in iron content from volcanic activity about 2.5 million years ago.

Over time the ocean currents have swept these sands north from near Taranaki and deposited them along the coastline.

The iron-sand deposit at Tahāroa, south of Kāwhia Harbour, is the largest in New Zealand, with an estimated reserve of 300 million tonnes.

Mined sand is used to make steel.

WEST COAST

PIHA
TE PIHA | LION ROCK

Looming large over the beach, this slab of rock is an eroded 16 million-year-old volcanic neck that provides the perfect vantage point for nearly 360-degree views of this coastal surfing mecca.

INFORMATION

GRADE: Medium/Hard

ACCESSIBILITY: Steep rocky steps.

TIME: 30 min return.

FACILITIES: Toilets halfway along North Piha Road, and by the main beach.

LOCATION: Plenty of parking beside the beach.

DOGS: On leads.

Don't be put off by the first jagged rocky section. The steps and pathway do get a little smoother, although no less vertical!

There are sensational coastal views as the path twists its way up the spine of the outcrop. The rock separates the two main beaches, Piha Beach and North Piha Beach.

You can't climb to the very top but you can walk to a handy seat from where you can plot your next adventure. Climbing any further is extremely dangerous due to rockfall and cliffs.

The pou (land-marker post) is dedicated to Te Kawerau ā Maki, the iwi of the west coast's ancestress Ngāti Tangiaro Taua, who loved this spot.

On the slow, careful descent, you'll receive a bird's-eye view of the small township and Piha Stream as it meanders its way to the coast.

MĀORI HISTORY

The important defensive Whakaari pā was perched on Lion Rock and was occupied by Te Kawerau ā Maki. There were several pā sites located on the headlands near Piha – including Te Wahangū at the north end of the beach. The main pā was situated on the ridge above the lagoon and called Maungaroa. The area is peppered with midden sites (domestic rubbish heaps), terraces and cave shelters from Māori settlement. There are terraces and pits still visible near the top of Te Piha.

IMPORTANT

Little kids will struggle on some of the steps and, naturally, keep an eye on all kids as the drop-offs are unforgiving. There are safety handrails for the majority of the climb.

119

WEST COAST

PIHA
KITEKITE FALLS

These falls are perched at the end of a rainforest valley dotted with regenerating kauri trees, after timber-milling fever swept through the area in the 1900s.

Bring the family and edge through a palm-shrouded valley on raised boardwalks and stairs installed to protect the roots of kauri trees growing nearby. There's a gradual slope as you follow the Glen Esk Stream through regenerating rainforest to the junction with the Knutzen Track.

Perhaps take a one-minute detour on the signposted Connect Track to see whether you'd be comfortable crossing the stream here, which is an option on your return. If not, just return on the Knutzen Track after exploring the waterfall.

The well-graded trail continues, and you'll get plenty of views of the upcoming tiered waterfall through the trees. There are also some vantage points to see above the falls where the unsuccessful Glen Esk Dam was built.

The final push to the waterfall involves crossing a small rocky stream before you can relax beside the rock pool and admire the 40-metre falls. The pool is perfect for kids to have a paddle. You can return on the Connect Track and cross the stream, or return the same way you came.

There's a 10-minute side track to the top of the falls.

The waterfall is also known as Kitakita Falls and Ketekete Falls.

MILLING HISTORY

Glen Esk Dam was built above the waterfall in about 1910. It was designed as a driving dam to hold kauri logs before they were released over the waterfall and transported to Piha Mill. However, when the first batch of logs plummeted into the pool below, they smashed into small pieces. The dam was not used for that purpose again.

BYERS WALK

On your return, take the first bridge on your right onto the signposted Byers Walk which takes you through a lush palm grove to a massive rata looming over the pathway and a small glade. Cross another bridge to reconnect with the main track. The detour

WEST COAST

doesn't add any extra time on your return trip.

This buggy-friendly option is also a good mini-adventure if you don't want to walk to the falls. It'll take about 15 minutes return, but you'll need to navigate the kauri dieback washing station at the start of the trail.

> **INFORMATION**
>
> GRADE: Medium
>
> ACCESSIBILITY: Boardwalks, steps, well-graded dirt paths and stream crossings.
>
> TIME: 1 hour (about 3 km) for a quick return trip.
>
> FACILITIES: Accessible public toilets and picnic tables.
>
> LOCATION: Parking at the end of Glenesk Road.
>
> DOGS: On leads.

WEST COAST

PIHA
TASMAN LOOKOUT PATH AND THE GAP

If there's one walk to do at Piha, this is it. It takes you to a vantage point over the entire beach, before dropping down into a secluded cove where huge, frothy waves thrash against exposed cliffs.

Head to the southern end of Piha Beach and follow the sign up the steps. Ignore the gut-busting beginning of this trail – it'll be over before you know it!

The trail skirts a couple of rocky outcrops, and if you need an excuse to stop for a breather, there are plenty of photo-worthy views of Lion Rock through the shrubbery.

At the top, turn right to the Tasman Lookout and join the masses enjoying the view. If you look south to Puaotetai Bay, you'll see where you'll be returning on the sand as part of the loop track.

Don't fancy the full loop? Just head back the way you came. Allow 20 minutes return to Tasman Lookout. If you're keen to tackle the loop, backtrack to the junction and keep walking.

The path meanders past flax and cabbage trees then descends through low coastal vegetation to a vantage point overlooking The Gap.

The Gap is famous in Piha. It's where the tide surges through a narrow low point between Taitomo Island and the cliffs opposite. At the turning of the tide, the incoming waves create a raging display before splaying out into the small cove. It's impressive to see at all times but particularly in big surf.

Continue down the steps, and you'll come out at Puaotetai Bay, near The Gap, where you can eyeball nature's power from sea level. The bush-clad hills surrounding this cove makes it feel wonderfully isolated – despite a hive of activity just around the corner on Piha Beach.

Near low tide, the waves create the placid Blue Pool where kids can safely take a dip.

From here, follow your nose back towards Piha Beach. Peer through the tidal tunnel The Keyhole at the base of Taitomo Island (which means 'the passageway of the sea') and watch the rolling surf speckled with wetsuit-clad surfers catching a wave.

WEST COAST

If the tide is in, the last section includes a scramble over rocks. Little kids will need a helping hand here. Take your time and don't miss peering into the rock pools.

IMPORTANT
The rocky area immediately around The Gap is hazardous, as the waves are unpredictable.

INFORMATION

GRADE: Medium

ACCESSIBILITY: Dirt path, sand and steps.

TIME: 1 hour (about 2 km) for the loop.

FACILITIES: Toilets at Piha Beach.

LOCATION: Southern end of Piha Beach.

DOGS: No dogs allowed.

WEST COAST

PIHA
TE ĀHUA POINT | MERCER BAY PATH

This historic site is perched on a dramatic rocky headland jutting out into the Tasman Sea. If you dare, stand on the lookout dangling nearly 175 metres above the shoreline and imagine what life would have been like on this wild, windswept rock.

The first lookout gives you a bird's-eye view of Te Āhua Point, which was home to a small pā occupied in the mid- to late 15th century. Its difficult location has perplexed researchers, because settlements historically were positioned closer to accessible food sources by beaches and rivers. Perhaps Māori settled here because the site was easily defended, which would make it one of the country's first fortified villages. Or, based on the evidence that at least one tsunami battered the area in the 1400s, Māori may have decided to stay on higher ground.

Ancestors of Te Kawerau ā Maki (the iwi of the west coast) say the headland was chosen because it was close to Hikurangi, the highest hill nearby. Archaeological digs at Te Āhua Pā have unearthed bone fish hooks, stone flakes from adze manufacture and chert drill points (chert is a hard sedimentary rock). Unearthed middens (domestic rubbish heaps) filled with fish bones indicate that snapper, blue moki and trevally would have been on the menu, along with tītī/muttonbirds.

The final lookout has views over the Tasman Sea. To the south, you can see the enormous wetlands and dunes at Whatipū. Keep an eye on the kids, as the path does pass some unfenced cliff edges.

MERCER BAY

Andrew Mercer received the cliff-locked bay as a Crown grant in 1866. But its remote and windswept location meant he moved on relatively quickly.

The Lovetts and the Usshers later farmed the bay.

WWII RADAR STATION

Near the car park, there are remnants of a WWII radar station. The high cliffs surrounding the headland provided additional security. The information panels share some of the crew's pranks!

NATURE DISCOVERY

SPOT THE DIFFERENCE
GECKO OR SKINK?

New Zealand has more than 100 species of geckos and skinks which are not found anywhere else. Here are some of their differences so you can tell them apart.

- Geckos have loose, velvety skin that looks one size too large. Skinks are smooth-skinned, sleek and shiny, with small legs.
- Geckos' eyes are large, and they can't blink. They have to clean their eyes with their tongue! Skinks blink.
- When geckos shed their skin it comes off in one go, or in large pieces. Skinks rub their skin off in small patches.
- Geckos have big, round toes with pads covered in microscopic hairs. These hairs give them the ability to climb, even upside down on a ceiling. Skinks have very slender toes and don't have the same toe pads.
- Geckos can vocalise. Many of our species make a chirping sound.

Top: Coromandel striped gecko (Image © Thomas David Miles ZOOM-OLOGY.com). Above: Common skink.
Text © Waikato Regional Council.

TO LOOP OR NOT?

The path loops back to the car park up a steep hill with limited views. Little kids will struggle with the climb. Save the tears, skip the signposted loop and head back the way you came.

INFORMATION

GRADE: Medium

ACCESSIBILITY: Well-graded paths with some steep sections and steps.

TIME: 1 hour (about 2 km) return.

FACILITIES: Toilet at the car park.

LOCATION: Turn off Piha Road onto Te Ahuahu Road which turns into Log Race Road. The last section is gravel.

DOGS: On leads.

WEST COAST
KAREKARE BEACH

Craggy cliffs dominate the landscape and create mystical reflections in the water at high tide. The beach was made famous as the setting for the New Zealand film *The Piano*.

Escape the masses and head to Karekare Beach with its converging streams that little kids will love paddling in. Walk along the beach, soak up the brisk fresh air and return home with sand between your toes. Because of its relative isolation, this beach doesn't have many facilities, so best to come prepared. However, Piha is just down the road if you need supplies or coffee. There's a picnic area beside the car park with some shade, and it's near the toilets. Tucked up in the nearby hills are the homes of some of New Zealand's most famous artists.

THE PIANO

Karekare Beach is a popular spot for movie buffs after it featured in the 1993 film *The Piano*, directed by Jane Campion. It starred Holly Hunter as Ada, as well as Sam Neill and Anna Paquin, who won an Academy Award for her performance aged just 11 years old. The beach provided a backdrop to where Ada's beloved piano was initially abandoned.

MĀORI HISTORY

This area was settled as early as 1150 by Te Kawerau ā Maki, iwi who lived here peacefully until an attack on their pā/fortified village left only a lone survivor. The pā was built on the prominent outcrop called Te Kākā Whakaara, now known as The Watchman.

EARLY SETTLEMENT

European settlement began in 1845 when the farming Shaw brothers, their wives and 24 children arrived. They also tackled the arduous task of creating the steep road known as The Cutting. Later, Charles Murdoch bought out the family and built a mill to process the 100,000 feet (around 30,480 metres) of timber cut each week. In 1900, Charles and Maria Farley purchased the property and offered luxury accommodation at Winchelsea House. This enterprising duo used a flume (a man-made water channel) to generate electricity for their guests, a decade before Auckland had electricity in homes.

NATURE DISCOVERY

INFORMATION

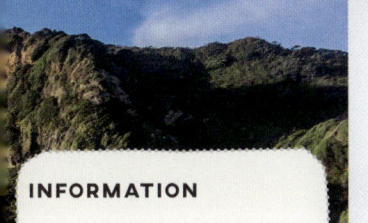

GRADE: Easy

ACCESSIBILITY: Lots of hot black sand! So, bring shoes for all the family.

TIME: Allow a couple of hours to explore the beach and take in the waterfalls.

FOOD OUTLETS: Bring plenty of water and snacks. There are no shops at the beach.

RUBBISH: Pack out all your rubbish, including leftovers.

GETTING THERE: From Titirangi Village take Scenic Drive and follow the signs towards Piha. The turn-off to Karekare Beach is well signposted before Piha.

DOGS: Dogs on leads are allowed on the beach and nearby tracks. They are prohibited on Whatipū Beach, south of Karekare Point.

FACILITIES: Toilet by the car park.

IMPORTANT: Don't forget your sunscreen and hat!

ROAD ACCESS: The road down to Karekare Beach is narrow and winding and not suitable for large vehicles, as there's a large pōhutukawa tree which overhangs the road, reducing the height clearance to about 3 metres.

THIS BEACH HAS STRONG RIPS AND CURRENTS, LARGE WAVES AND DEEP HOLES. LIFEGUARDS PATROL THE BEACH ONLY WHEN THE YELLOW AND RED FLAGS ARE DISPLAYED. ALWAYS SWIM BETWEEN THE FLAGS.

HAVE YOU SEEN A
BIRD OF PREY?

New Zealand has three native raptors. The term 'raptor' comes from the Latin word 'rapere', which means 'to snatch or take away'. These birds use their feet to catch their prey, and their hooked beak helps them eat bite-sized pieces of their catch.

KĀREAREA | NEW ZEALAND FALCON

Falcons are capable of flying at speeds over 100 kilometres an hour and are often seen flying in active chase rather than slowly swooping around like the harrier. They kill their prey with a quick bite to the neck, and their diet mainly consists of birds but also insects.

KĀHU | SWAMP HARRIER

Harriers like to feed on road kill and are often spotted perched on roadside fences. Possums, rabbits and hedgehogs make up a large part of their diet. They are opportunistic hunters while flying lazily and are the country's largest bird of prey.

RŪRŪ | MOREPORK

By day they roost in the cavities of trees, and at night they hunt for beetles, wētā, moths and spiders. At dusk, you can often hear their haunting call, and during the night they can be heard in many urban parks and leafy suburbs.

WEST COAST

KAREKARE BEACH
PŌHUTUKAWA GLADE WALK

When the gnarly pōhutukawa trees are flowering, this walk passes under masses of fiery red blooms. But even outside of summer, kids will love the wizened trees bending over the path – a spot of tree climbing, anyone?

This kid-friendly little jaunt takes in all the highlights of the dramatic windswept Karekare Beach and the trees filter the summer rays to provide some mid-day respite.

From the main car park, walk south over the small bridge and you'll spy signs to the glade a little further along on your right. Ignore the first path to the beach.

After exploring the pōhutukawa trees, there's a picnic table and a small glade where kids can kick around a ball or play Frisbee.

The trail slowly transforms from a dirt trail into a sandy path through rolling dunes. You'll hear the roar of the ocean before you round the final corner and see Paratahi Island perched in the surf.

To complete the loop, walk north along the beach towards Company Stream. On wild, windy days when the sand is whipped up, you'll receive a free body scrub! From near the little stream, you can follow the path through the dunes back to the bridge near the car park.

INFORMATION

GRADE: Easy

ACCESSIBILITY: Road, dirt and sand paths, and beach.

TIME: 45 min to 1 hour (about 2 km) to complete the loop.

FACILITIES: Toilet at the car park.

LOCATION: Main car park at Karekare Beach.

DOGS: On leads.

PŌHUTUKAWA TREES

Pōhutukawa (*Metrosideros excelsa*) are fondly known as the New Zealand Christmas tree, which is about the time of year when they erupt into an impressive crimson display.

However, the tree is a tasty treat for possums, which eat many of them to death.

Young pōhutukawa grow at about 30cm per year in height and 5-10mm in diameter (thickness), while older trees grow about 10cm a year and only 2mm in diameter.

FIND OUT MORE
projectcrimson.org.nz

WEST COAST

The dunes are home to many native birds, including tūturiwhatu/New Zealand dotterel, pīhoihoi/New Zealand pipit and karoro/southern black-backed gulls.

Allow more time if you're picnicking, or planning to walk out to Paratahi Island at low tide and wander south to explore the rock pools.

MĀORI HISTORY

Paratahi Island is also known in Māori history as Te Tokapaoke. It's considered 'the sibling who stands alone' after straying too far from its mother Te Kākā Whakaara/The Watchman, which is the sharp rocky outcrop at the northernmost end of the beach.

NATURE DISCOVERY

IDENTIFY
NATIVE BIRDS

Keep your ears open and eyes peeled for these birds which call New Zealand home.

1. PĪWAKAWAKA FANTAIL

Take a peek behind you while exploring because these friendly birds often follow along checking the disturbed soil for tasty bugs. Listen out for its friendly 'cheet cheet', and hopefully they'll put on a very energetic flying display for you. Look for their distinctive fanned tail as they dart around. They are known for being quite vocal, except when it is particularly cold.

2. KERERŪ | NEW ZEALAND PIGEON

These big birds are very quiet except when they crash-land in the trees! Only occasionally will you hear them let loose a soft 'oo'. Importantly, they spread the seed of more than 70 native forest plants. They are widespread throughout New Zealand and on some forested/shrubby offshore islands.

3. TŪĪ | PARSON BIRD

Tūī enjoy feasting on nectar but when that is scarce, they feed on fruit and insects. Around September and October, you may see them diving and duet singing when they're courting their mate. Tūī are found nowhere else in the world.

4. WHITEHEAD PŌPOKOTEA

Found in flocks high in the forest canopy, where they are on the hunt for spiders, moths and beetles. They can often be seen hanging upside down while feeding! Their tuneful calls are common in North Island beech forests, podocarp forest and old-growth exotic plantation forests. They are about 15 centimetres long and have black beaks and eyes.

5. MIROMIRO | TOMTIT

These small birds are about 13 centimetres long and weigh only 11 grams. The oldest known miromiro was 16 years old, which is impressive because the average life expectancy is only three years. Look out for their bulky nests in tree forks. Tomtits often perch on a branch or cling to a trunk while scanning for prey, before swiftly flying down to snatch it.

6. KŌTARE | SACRED KINGFISHER

These unique birds are often spotted in elevated spots, including the tops of fence posts or telephone wires, which lets them spy on their dinner. Their calls are rather unmusical! They use their bill to chisel out nests in cliffs, banks and cuttings. Near estuaries they mainly eat small crabs while in open country they munch on cicadas, beetles, wētā, small lizards and mice.

WEST COAST

KAREKARE BEACH
KAREKARE FALLS AND OPAL POOLS STREAM CASCADE

This 30-metre 'horsetail' waterfall flows off the ranges and plunges into a fern-shrouded pool – which makes you feel like you're taking a dip in a secluded tropical oasis.

INFORMATION

GRADE: Easy

ACCESSIBILITY: Dirt paths.

TIME: 20 min return for a quick explore.

FACILITIES: Toilet at the car park.

LOCATION: Main car park at Karekare Beach.

DOGS: On leads.

From the car park, head south over the small bridge and walk up the road about 100 metres, then follow the signpost to Taraire Track on your left.

The easy trail continues between massive boulders and beneath palm trees before the main attraction appears. In warm weather, grab the togs and wade into the pool for some fun family wallowing.

Despite not being on the main tourist trail, this waterfall on Company Stream does still pull the crowds as a picturesque selfie backdrop. But generally, there's plenty of space around the pool to lay out a blanket and enjoy a picnic.

OPAL POOLS STREAM CASCADE

On the way to Karekare Falls, you'll pass the equally pretty Opal Pools Stream Cascade which offers kids a free-for-all opportunity to clamber over a wide waterfall. Older kids will easily reach the top pools to dip their toes in.

If you're heading home late in the day, the huge pōhutukawa trees lining the trail are often bathed in golden light.

131

WEST COAST
WHATIPŪ BEACH

This vast, windswept black-sand beach curves around the entrance to Manukau Harbour. It's the most remote of all the Auckland's west coast beaches and offers a less populated outing than its northern neighbours.

Poke around in the cliff caves, and if the conditions are right, you can scramble over the rocks on Paratūtae Island. There is an easily accessible beach from the car park which would suit little legs, or you can make it a more extensive outing and walk past Ninepin Rock to access the long western beach which stretches to Karekare Beach. On a blustery day, the wind whips the sand up and down the coast – impressive! You may even spot a kororā/little penguin or lumbering rāpoka/sea lion taking a breather on the beach.

SCIENTIFIC RESERVE
This headland is a Department of Conservation scientific reserve managed by Auckland Council. There is a range of habitats including freshwater wetlands and saltmarsh vegetation that are home to threatened native species. Tūturiwhatu/New Zealand dotterel breed here so take care to follow the established paths. Local iwi recall a sizeable flat-sand island offshore called Parore; however, over time, the island disappeared.

MĀORI HISTORY
Whatipū was a strategic vantage point, and the abundant kaimoana/seafood nearby attracted early Māori settlement. The frost-free valley also meant kūmara flourished. Remnants of pā sites/fortified villages, terraces for homes and shell middens (domestic rubbish heaps) suggest Whatipū was occupied for some time. Fish, seal and whale bones have been found in middens nearby as well. Stranded whales would have provided a significant amount of food for Māori, and the bones could be shaped into tools and ornaments.

TIMBER MILLING
For two decades from 1866 the beach was the hub of an impressive kauri timber milling business run by the Gibbons family, who was originally from Newfoundland. Kauri was common in the valley, and a wooden tramway transported the logs to a wharf beside Paratūtae Island.

WEST COAST

INFORMATION

GRADE: Easy

ACCESSIBILITY: Lots of hot black sand! Can be a little boggy near the dunes.

TIME: Allow a couple of hours to explore the beach and have a picnic. More if exploring the nearby Whatipū Caves (p135).

FOOD OUTLETS: Bring plenty of water and snacks. There are no shops near the beach.

RUBBISH: Pack out all your rubbish, including leftovers.

GETTING THERE: Drive through Titirangi Village and follow Huia Road until it changes to Whatipū Road. Plenty of parking at the end. The last section is well-graded gravel. At the fork, turn left.

DOGS: No dogs allowed – very important because of the nesting wildlife.

FACILITIES: Toilet by the car park.

IMPORTANT: Don't forget your sunscreen and hat!

SWIMMING IS NOT ADVISABLE BECAUSE OF STRONG RIPS, LARGE WAVES, DEEP HOLES AND CURRENTS. LIFEGUARDS DO NOT PATROL THIS BEACH.

HUIA POINT LOOKOUT

Don't miss this short detour if you're heading out to the West Coast for an adventure.

This small lookout offers panoramic views across the harbour to Manukau Heads and the northern tip of Āwhitu Peninsula.

Despite nearly 10 million years' worth of silt smothering its seabed, the Manukau Harbour has an impressive tidal variation of up to 4 metres. So, you can visit on your way to Whatipū Beach, then on your return you can see a completely different landscape.

Because of the harbour's important historical transport routes and plentiful kaimoana/seafood, many Māori pā sites/fortified villages were built on the shoreline. During European settlement, vast tracts of bush on the surrounding hills were logged for kauri, which was then shipped from a wharf at Whatipū Beach.

HUIA

Huia was named after the extinct huia bird. Deforestation of its habitat for pasture and rampant overhunting for its skin to mount contributed to its extinction. Its tail feathers were also prized for decorating hats. Although there were reported sightings in the 1960s, the last official confirmed sighting of a huia was in 1907. The magpie-sized bird was the largest of the five New Zealand wattlebird species and was widespread throughout the North Island but absent from the South Island. It had a deep metallic, bluish-black plumage.

GETTING THERE

Turn left off Huia Road (near No. 1077) onto Huia Point Lookout Road. Allow five to ten minutes. Dogs on leads.

NATURE DISCOVERY

KEEP AN EYE OPEN FOR
MARINE ANIMALS

Ever wondered how to tell a sea lion and fur seal apart? Sea lions have blunt noses, short whiskers and are found on or near sandy beaches. Fur seals are smaller and have pointy noses, and are often found on rocky shorelines. But always keep your distance from both!

BOTTLENOSE DOLPHIN

SHORT-BEAKED COMMON DOLPHIN

RĀPOKA
NEW ZEALAND SEA LION

KEKENO
NEW ZEALAND FUR SEAL

MAKI | ORCA
KILLER WHALE

MANGŌ TANIWHA | GREAT WHITE SHARK

WHATIPŪ BEACH
WHATIPŪ BEACH SEA CAVES

These ancient sea caves were once the spot for high-spirited dances during the height of the settlement's timber-milling days, and are now the stomping ground for intrepid explorers.

INFORMATION

GRADE: Easy/Medium

ACCESSIBILITY: At times rough, narrow dirt path. Boggy in winter.

TIME: 1 hour (3 km) return.

FACILITIES: Toilet by the car park.

LOCATION: Start by the information shelter at Whatipū Beach car park and follow the signs beside the camping area.

DOGS: No dogs allowed.

From the car park, the path heads north to the base of the cliffs and edges past a handful of accessible caves. The undulating track provides views over the wetlands to the Tasman Sea and further north to Karekare Beach.

The largest cave, Te Ana Ru/The Ballroom, was once a dance hall that hosted formal dances for more than 60 years from the early 1900s. Keen dancers tackled the relatively inhospitable roads by horseback, or by boat from Onehunga, to reach the lamplit cave decorated with ribbons and native ferns. Partygoers mingled while an accordion band belted out popular tunes. The cave's kauri dance floor might still be buried deep under the sand. While you're there, test out the impressive echoes or take along your musical instruments for an impromptu band session.

IMPORTANT

Take a torch to explore all the nooks and crannies in the caves – but be careful, as rockfall does occur near the cave mouths.

SPIRULA SPIRULA RAM'S HORN SQUID

These distinctive white coiled shells are an internal buoyancy aid for spirula spirula – also known as the ram's horn squid.

These little critters are about 35 to 45 millimetres long but are rarely seen because they are deep-water dwellers.

However, their internal shells are common on beaches.

If you crush the shell, you'll see the small chambers that the squid fills with air so it can rise and descend in deep water.

WAITĀKERE RANGES

WAITĀKERE RANGES

BUSH-CLAD
WAITĀKERE RANGES

Head west to explore adventures on the flanks of an ancient volcano, and climb up to lookouts perched high above the Manukau Harbour.

HIGHLIGHTS

TAKE A QUICK STROLL TO A MASSIVE KAURI TREE WHICH SURVIVED THE RAVAGES OF TIMBER MILLING.

This kauri is one of the biggest in the Waitākere Ranges Regional Park and is worth a quick stop if you're driving past (p139).

THE UPPER NIHOTUPU DAM IS A CROWD-PLEASER FOR ALL AGES; A DAM, WATERFALLS, VAST RESERVOIR AND A HISTORIC RAILWAY.

The dam is shrouded in forest and has some great highlights to make it a memorable half-day adventure (p140).

NEED TO BRUSH UP ON YOUR BOTANICAL KNOWLEDGE? HEAD TO THE PLANT ID LOOP NEAR ARATAKI VISITOR CENTRE.

This kid-friendly loop has plenty of native plant signs to help school you up on all the New Zealand flora you've ever pondered over (p145).

SAVE OUR KAURI FORESTS
They are dying from kauri dieback disease

It spreads by soil movement
ACT NOW to help stop it

ALWAYS

1. SCRUB YOUR GEAR
Remove soil before AND after forest visits – scrub your shoes, tyres and equipment

2. STAY ON THE TRACK
AND off kauri roots

KEEP KAURI STANDING
STOP KAURI DIEBACK DISEASE SPREADING | KIA TOITU HE KAURI

www.kauridieback.co.nz

TĀNGATA WHENUA | MINISTRY FOR PRIMARY INDUSTRIES | DEPARTMENT OF CONSERVATION | NORTHLAND REGIONAL COUNCIL | AUCKLAND COUNCIL | WAIKATO REGIONAL COUNCIL | BAY OF PLENTY REGIONAL COUNCIL

KD012 March 2019

Ko Tātou This Is Us

BIOSECURITY 2025

WAITĀKERE RANGES

WAIATARUA
LARGE KAURI WALK

No surprises here! This aptly named adventure delivers an impressive mighty kauri for you to marvel at its size. It's such a treat to see one of the world's longest-living trees, with so little effort.

This kauri is one of the biggest in the Waitākere Ranges Regional Park and is worth a quick stop if you're driving past. It will only take a couple of minutes.

The 30-metre-long trail deposits you at a viewing platform where you can peer skyward into the kauri, which has branches laden with thriving epiphytes.

The Waitākere Ranges was teeming with these mighty natives until kauri timber fever swept the nation in the late 1700s to 1800s. Bushmen with teams of bullocks and large-scale mills decimated the region's kauri forests by 1900.

European settlers used the straight timber in ships' masts and house building, and varnish manufacturers used the kauri gum.

IMPORTANT
Take extreme care crossing the road, as cars often speed around the blind corner.

INFORMATION

GRADE: Easiest

ACCESSIBILITY: Dirt path and steps.

TIME: 5 min return.

FACILITIES: None.

LOCATION: 600 Scenic Drive, Waitākere.

DOGS: No dogs allowed.

KAHAKAHA PERCHING LILY

These epiphytes nestle in the crooks of the trees where humus (soil formed by decomposing leaves and other plant material) has accumulated over time. Early European bushmen called them 'Widowmakers' because they often fell from milled trees. It was not life-extending to be under a massive specimen as it plummeted to the ground! The young plant has a classic fan shape and often grows in large colonies in forest tree branches. Also known as a tank lily.

Image: Bruce Calvert / CC-BY

WAITĀKERE RANGES
UPPER NIHOTUPU DAM

This dam is such a cool forest adventure for families. There's so much to see – everything from a dam, waterfalls, to a vast reservoir and a historic railway.

INFORMATION

GRADE: Medium

ACCESSIBILITY: Well-graded paths.

TIME: 1 hour (about 5 km) return to the top of the dam; 1 hour 30 min (about 7.5 km) return along the tramline to the base of the dam.

FACILITIES: Rustic toilet near the car park or a more modern option beside the picnic area.

LOCATION: Piha Road.

DOGS: On leads.

From the car park, stroll through the native bush and along a well-graded four-wheel-drive track to the top of the first waterfall, which has some interesting rock formations to explore. Watch out for the steep ledges, though.

Another waterfall further down the hill is the start of the winding canyon that opens up to the broad reservoir. A small trail takes you to the waterfall where kids can poke around by the moss-covered rocks and small pool.

The path then winds around the reservoir's edge towards the dam. When water levels are low, the golden-coloured dirt banks appear above the water, in stark contrast to the overhanging forest.

From the top of the wide-lipped dam, you can peer down the forested valley, and back across the reservoir to the ridgeline where you started from.

If the legs still have some juice in them, continue walking downhill to the picnic area, which is pretty although it doesn't have any great views. Then, follow the unused tramline through lush rainforest to the base of the dam where there's a small lookout. Peer up at the water cascading down the dam's concrete spillway. When it's in full flow, be prepared for a good dose of spray!

This path is doable with outdoorsy buggies but you'll need to navigate the kauri dieback station. Be prepared for a bit of a slog back up the gravel path.

THE DAM

After heavy rain, the reservoir and spillway control the flow of water released to prevent flooding downstream. Throughout the year, the spillway also does controlled releases to maintain natural flora and fauna habitats.

The Waitākere (nearly 5,000 hectares) and Huia (almost 10,000 hectares) catchments collect about three-quarters of Auckland's water, which the dams store before piping it to water treatment plants, then onto showers and taps across the city.

WAITĀKERE RANGES

The sand and cement used to construct the dam was transported from Onehunga by barge across the Manukau Harbour, then hauled 4 kilometres on a tramline up the valley, before a locomotive delivered the materials to the worksite.

DAM FACTS

The concrete dam took eight years to build and was completed in 1923. It's 218.5 metres above sea level and has a catchment area of 999 hectares.

GETTING THERE

From Waiatarua (near the top of the Waitākere Ranges) take Piha Road and head west for approximately 5 minutes. Parking available on the left; this does fill up during weekends and school holidays so you may have to park on the road.

WAITĀKERE RANGES

WAITĀKERE RANGES
ARATAKI VISITOR CENTRE

Are you heading west? Pop into this excellent visitor centre for stunning views of the surrounding rainforest, and to learn about the rich Māori history of the mighty Waitākere Ranges.

Billed as the gateway to the Waitākere Ranges, this visitor centre has a series of balconies where you can take in the area's rugged natural beauty. Take a peek through the large binoculars over the reservoirs and out to the Manukau Harbour. Arataki means 'place of learning' in te reo Māori.

Inside, there's a kids' educational corner with black-sand magnets, puzzles, puppets and a microscope, and a range of nature books to purchase. Outside, take a selfie within the gilded frame overlooking the forest — perhaps while chomping down on ice cream from the pop-up café. Information panels by the car park show how Scenic Drive was built during the 1930s. Harrowing times!

WAITĀKERE RANGES
The Ranges are the remnants of an extinct undersea volcano which formed about 22 million years ago, called the Waitākere Volcano. The massive volcano was the size of Lake Taupō and could have been between 3,000 and 4,000 metres high. It formed about 20 kilometres off the coast of Piha and intermittently erupted until about 16 million years ago, when it was forced out of the sea. Then, about five million years ago, major earth movements pushed up the volcano's eastern flank, which is the present-day Ranges with its razor-back ridges and deep valleys. Ongoing erosion by the Tasman Sea and earth movements have removed all visible parts of the volcano above sea level off the west coast.

The forest is regenerating after extensive logging and farming tore through the landscape from the mid-1800s. The forest is now home to a variety of native flora and fauna as well as critters including kauri snails, wētā, Hochstetter's frog and pekapeka-tōu-roa/long-tailed bats.

KAURI DIEBACK
Many walks in the Ranges have been closed to prevent the spread of the incurable kauri dieback disease. At the time of writing, the walks in this guidebook were open to the public. The visitor centre has

WAITĀKERE RANGES

free maps that indicate all closures, or tracks that have reopened after preventative track maintenance.

INFORMATION

OPENING HOURS: 9am to 5pm every day. Closed Christmas Day. The car park is open from 6am to 9pm in summer and between 6am and 7pm in winter.

FACILITIES: Toilets and picnic tables.

LOCATION: 300 Scenic Drive, Oratia, Waitākere.

DOGS: On leads by the visitor centre.

WAITĀKERE RANGES
LOWER NIHOTUPU DAM

After exploring the Upper Nihotupu Dam (p140), head south to Parau for a mini-adventure by the lower reservoir. See if you can spot any overflow rushing down the dam's crest from the lookout next to the car park.

Grab an ice cream in Huia before visiting this reservoir which is handily very close to the road.

It was the fourth of five dams built within the Waitākere Ranges to supply water to Auckland, and covers an area of nearly 53 hectares and has a capacity of 4.6 million cubic metres. During WWII there was a spike in water usage, primarily from the establishment of several military bases, two airfields and hospitals for US troops. At that time the two bases were churning through more than 3.2 million litres of water every day.

Construction of this dam began in 1945 and took three years. It was the first in the country to be built using roller-compacted earth instead of the more traditional concrete dams. It's 24.7 metres high and has a crest length of 381 metres. When the water just starts to spill over the lip of the dam, it looks like intricate lace.

INFORMATION

GRADE: Easiest

ACCESSIBILITY: Grass and concrete.

TIME: 5 min.

FACILITIES: None.

LOCATION: Small car park located near 592 Huia Road, Parau.

DOGS: On leads.

NATURE DISCOVERY

IDENTIFY
NATIVE TREES

While out and about adventuring, how many of these native trees can you recognise?

1. KAURI

This magnificent towering tree is one of the world's longest-living trees – they can live for more than 2,000 years! But their survival is at risk from the incurable kauri dieback disease. The world's tallest kauri is the 51-metre-high Tāne Māhuta 'Lord of the Forest' in Waipoua Forest, Northland. Kauri timber was used by Māori for boat building and carving. The gum was used as a fire starter.

2. CABBAGE TREE TĪ KŌUKA

Early New Zealand settlers used the trunks of these trees as chimneys in their huts because they are remarkably fire resistant. The tree was also planted on the boundaries of important locations. They can grow from 12 to 20 metres high and the long, narrow leaves (which can be used as kindling) can be up to 1 metre long.

3. KAHIKATEA

These trees existed during the Jurassic period. Flying dinosaurs probably swooped down and munched on their fleshy seeds! It's our tallest native tree (growing up to 60 metres high) and often pokes through the forest canopy. The tree is common near rivers and in swamp forests. Māori used soot from burning the heartwood to create pigment for tā moko/traditional tattooing.

4. RIMU

When mature, these conifers can soar to more than 50 metres high and live for 800 years. This non-flowering tree has long, draping needles that are prickly to touch, and brown bark with flaky strips. It produces seeds only every 5-6 years. It was commonly known as red pine, and was used to build homes and furniture.

5. TŌTARA

Māori used stone tools to carve massive waka from tōtara trunks – often taking more than a year to complete them. The rot-resistant wood was used for many purposes by Europeans, including railway sleepers and fence posts. This slow-growing tree reaches about 20 to 25 metres high. The largest known living tōtara, the Pouākani Tree, grows near Pureora in the central North Island.

6. PŪRIRI

These trees are an important food source for kererū/New Zealand pigeon, which also spread the tree's seeds. It is home to the caterpillar of New Zealand's largest moth, the pūriri moth, which drills a tunnel into the trunk. The average wingspan of the female moth is 15 centimetres. During pre-European times, Māori used the wood to make weapons and implements. The tree can grow to about 20 metres.

WAITĀKERE RANGES

KID-FRIENDLY STROLLS NEAR
ARATAKI VISITOR CENTRE

Spend half a day here exploring the little trails near the information centre; clamber up to the lookout with views over one of the city's key reservoirs, or tackle the Plant ID Loop and test out your plant-identification skills.

LOOKOUT

Don't miss this short walk to the lookout. It gives you a brilliant bird's-eye view of the Lower Nihotupu Reservoir (p143), which is one of five reservoirs in the Waitākere Ranges that supply water to Auckland. A short, steady uphill stroll beside a forested bank and along a boardwalk leads to the lookout. This vantage point also offers impressive views north and south – actually, everywhere! On a fine day, you'll be able to spot the Manukau Heads in the distance past Karangāhape Peninsula, which is also known as Cornwallis Peninsula.

GRADE: Easy

ACCESSIBILITY: Gravel path, steps and boardwalk.

TIME: 15 min (60 m) return.

LOCATION: The trail starts to the right of the visitor centre.

DOGS: On leads.

PLANT ID LOOP

This super kid-friendly loop starts beside Scenic Drive where you dip under the busy road through a tunnel decorated with murals. After the shelter, follow the signs off to the right – everything is well signposted. There are plenty of native plant signs to help school you up on all the New Zealand flora you've ever pondered over and discover plants that flourish in the Waitākere Ranges, including kawakawa and piupiu/crown fern, which lines the pathway. Towering palms create lush overhanging tunnels to stroll through on your return trip within the regenerating forest.

GRADE: Easy

ACCESSIBILITY: Concrete and gravel path suitable for buggies and assisted wheelchair users.

TIME: 20 min return to the visitor centre.

LOCATION: The trail starts on the other side of the pedestrian tunnel.

DOGS: On leads.

NATURE TRAIL – UPPER LOOP

This pleasant little loop has some steady slopes to test out little kids' resilience. It's outdoorsy-buggy friendly but you'll need to put in some grunt work on some of the inclines. The highlight of this walk is reaching the wooden lookout and peering through gaps in the forest to see the rolling, bush-clad hills of the Waitākere Ranges. Combine this walk with the Plant ID Loop and you'll spend a good hour soaking up the sights and learning about this area which traditionally was named Te Wao Nui o Tiriwa/The Great Forest of Tiriwā.

GRADE: Medium

ACCESSIBILITY: Concrete and gravel path suitable for buggies.

TIME: 30 min (2 km) return to the visitor centre.

LOCATION: The trail starts on the other side of the pedestrian tunnel.

DOGS: On leads.

AMBURY REGIONAL PARK

SOUTH AUCKLAND

HEAD TO
SOUTH AUCKLAND

Explore an internationally significant heritage landscape that provides an insight into some of the region's earliest Polynesian settlers, or visit a working farm and rub the noses of Clydesdale horses!

HIGHLIGHTS

IF YOU DARE, CLIMB THROUGH A DARK LAVA TUNNEL ON THE FORESHORE WALK.

Leave the farm animals behind at Ambury Regional Park and discover the fauna of the park's foreshore. This windswept stretch of coast hides some fun kid-friendly highlights (p152).

MĀNGERE MOUNTAIN ERUPTED IN A FIERY BLAST ABOUT 18,000 YEARS AGO.

From the top, you can see where the lava flowed from the crater and created vast lava fields. Now that things are a little calmer, it's home to docile cattle and camera-toting tourists (p149).

THE RUGGED ŌTUATAUA STONEFIELDS HISTORIC RESERVE WAS ONCE A BUSTLING GARDENING COMMUNITY.

The Auckland isthmus had 8,000 hectares of volcanic Stonefields but now just 160 hectares remain, which makes this sprawling site globally significant for its food cultivation history (p156).

SOUTH AUCKLAND

MĀNGERE BRIDGE
AMBURY REGIONAL PARK

This park juts out into the Manukau Harbour and is an intriguing blend of pastoral farming and natural intertidal mudflats. It may take a few trips to see all the sights in this unique landscape, which feels like a remote island.

Near the woolshed and milking shed, you can walk along the grassy lanes between the animal enclosures and watch the pigs, chickens, turkey, rabbits, goats – and possibly the elusive peacocks – go about their day.

Colin and Connor the Clydesdales are often spotted near the fence waiting for a friendly nose-scratching session.

In spring this farm explodes with an overwhelming dose of cuteness with baby lambs, piglets and calves tottering around on their new-found legs.

You can go free-range and wander around the animal enclosures, or take the signposted Ambury Farm Path. Both options take in the same sights, although kids might be keener to race off the track to see their favourite animals.

To get up close to the animals, you can enter the enclosures – except during lambing season from mid-July to early August. There are plenty of friendly signs to let you know what you can do around the animals. Just remember to leave gates as you found them.

After an explore, there are plenty of grassy spots to settle in for a picnic or barbecue – and challenge the kids to a few ball games.

MILKING
During winter you can watch the cows being milked daily at 10.30am in the Milking Shed.

FACILITIES
There are toilets and plenty of picnic tables beside the farm area. There are four barbecues available – two electric and two wood-burning (you'll need to bring wood). One of the electric barbecues is bookable. Camping sites are available too.

ACCESSIBILITY
The paths include gravel and grass which are suitable for outdoorsy buggies although they can get a little boggy in winter. Wheelchair users might struggle on some of the smaller paths.

SOUTH AUCKLAND

MĀNGERE BRIDGE
TE PANE A MATAAHO / MĀNGERE MOUNTAIN

This volcano last exploded in a fiery blast about 18,000 years ago. Rocks and plumes of steam mingled with rain, lightning and thunder while lava flowed from the crater and created vast lava fields. Now that it has calmed down, it's home to docile cattle and camera-toting tourists.

Walk around the perimeter or dip down into the crater then clamber up to the trig for views towards the Ōtuataua Stonefields and Te Motu a Hiaroa/Puketutu Island. Volcanic cones were hot-spots for early Polynesian settlement, and they provided commanding views which helped protect iwi from attack. Traditional crops like kūmara, taro and gourds flourished in the fertile warmer volcanic soils. You can still see the remnants of low stone walls that divided the landscape for gardens and living areas on this relatively unspoiled 106-metre-high cone.

INFORMATION

GRADE: Easy

ACCESSIBILITY: Well-graded dirt and grass paths.

TIME: 30 min (about 1 km) to explore the farm walk.

LOCATION: Ambury Road, Māngere Bridge.

DOGS: No dogs allowed in the main area. See the Auckland Council website for permitted areas.

INFORMATION

GRADE: Easy/Medium

ACCESSIBILITY: Easy if you walk around the perimeter. A bit more gut-busting if you dip down into the crater.

TIME: 45 min to 1 hour.

FACILITIES: Toilets by the sports fields. Playground and half-pipe.

LOCATION: Car park off Domain Road, Māngere Bridge.

DOGS: On leads.

149

SOUTH AUCKLAND

TOYOTA KIWI GUARDIANS
AMBURY REGIONAL PARK

This beautiful regional park has everything you need for an excellent family adventure. Discover farm animals to meet, fascinating volcanic history, heaps of birdlife and stunning views over the Manukau Harbour. The best part is that this park is not far from the heart of Auckland.

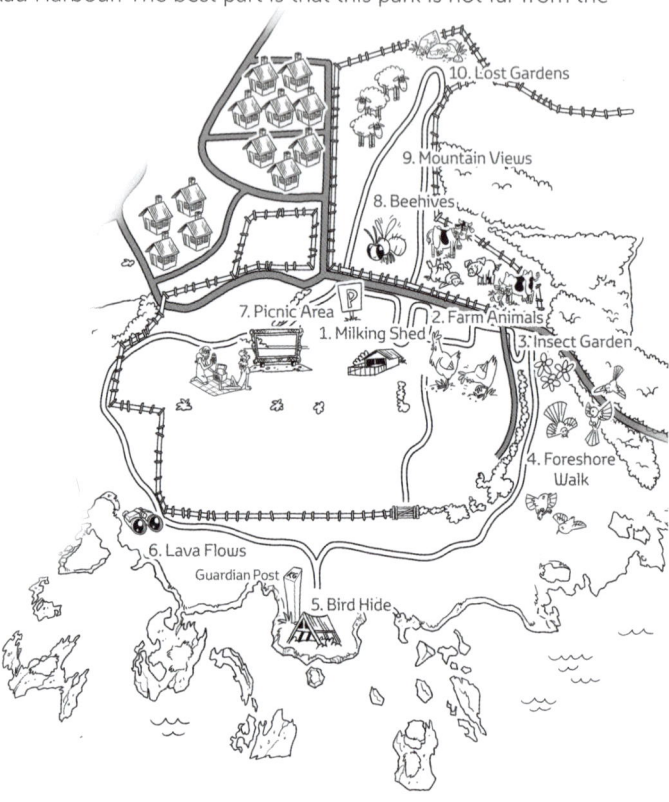

This adventure is part of the Toyota Kiwi Guardians programme. Before you visit, download an activity sheet from kiwiguardians.co.nz or use the one in this book. Claim a medal when you find the unique code written on the Kiwi Guardian Post.

1. MILKING SHED: Do you know how we get our milk from cows?

2. FARM ANIMALS: Oink oink! Meet the friendly farm animals. How many chickens, pigs and horses can you count?

3. INSECT GARDEN: Can you find any creepy crawlies hiding in the garden? They're very good at playing hide and seek, so look closely. Make sure you watch out for the ongaonga/stinging nettle!

4. FORESHORE WALK: Follow the yellow markers and see if you can hear the chirping birds. There are 86 bird species that live here – WOW! How many can you spot?

5. BIRD HIDE: Can you believe that some of these birds have flown all the way from Russia and Alaska to live here? Can you see any of them making their new homes?

SOUTH AUCKLAND

6. LAVA FLOWS: Ash and lava from volcanoes made the soil here perfect for growing plants. Which extinct volcanoes can you see from here?

7. PICNIC AREA: Time to stop and have a rest – we hope you packed a picnic. Make sure you get a photo in the giant photo frame before continuing your adventure.

8. BEEHIVES: Follow the blue marks, and you'll start to hear the sound of buzzing. Can you see any bees making honey in their hives? Be careful not to get stung.

9. MOUNTAIN VIEWS: Imagine hundreds of years ago when Māori lived around this maunga/mountain. Where do you think they lived?

10. LOST GARDENS: Make your way through the paddocks, and you'll see the stone mounds. What type of crops do you think Māori used to grow here?

Image and content courtesy of Toyota Kiwi Guardians.

INFORMATION

GRADE: Easy

ACCESSIBILITY: The entire walk is suitable only for walking. Bring sturdy footwear for this adventure. It might get muddy!

TIME: For points 1 to 7, allow 45 min (1 km). For points 8 to 10, allow 45 min (1 km).

LOCATION: Trail starts beside the Ambury Regional Park car park.

DOGS: No dogs allowed.

MĀNGERE BRIDGE
MĀNGERE LAGOON PATH

Māngere Mountain overshadows this volcanic maar (crater), which has an easy gravel path that loops around it. Ideal for a short escape outdoors.

An eruption blasted the crater's raised tuff ring into existence thousands of years ago and about 7,000 years ago it was breached by rising sea levels. The lagoon then filled with silt and mangroves and a land bridge formed across to the scoria cone protruding from the lake. Early settlers grazed their cattle on the exposed mound. The scoria cone was removed in the 1950s when earthworks dredged the lagoon to make way for sewage sludge ponds. When public demand prompted a land-based sewage treatment plant to be built nearby on the foreshore, the lagoon and scoria cone were restored in the early 2000s.

This path is not a tiring adventure, and if the flat loop isn't enough, you can head down to the shoreline and connect up with the Watercare Coastal Walkway (p154) to explore for longer. Or, spend some time beside the Mānukau Harbour looking at the wading birds which arrive from the Arctic Circle each year.

The wide gravel path is mostly dry and is suitable for buggies.

INFORMATION

GRADE: Easy

ACCESSIBILITY: Flat dirt and gravel paths.

TIME: 30 min (2.3 km) to walk the loop, or a 10-min bike ride.

LOCATION: Good starting point is on Creamery Road.

DOGS: No dogs allowed.

SOUTH AUCKLAND

MĀNGERE BRIDGE
AMBURY FORESHORE PATH

This often-windswept trail leads you to the edge of the vast Manukau Harbour, and if the kids are keen, they can clamber through lava caves created 18,000 years ago.

Leave the farm animals behind and follow the yellow markers from the end of the main car park, which lead to the farm's foreshore.

As you cross the open pasture, past the fenced-off freshwater wetland and native herb fields, look out for the roosting birds on the rocks or gathering food from the mudflats.

Keen bird-twitchers have identified more than 86 species of birds at Ambury. See if you can spy the threatened native ngutu pare/wrybill that has the only laterally-curved bill (always curved to the right) in the world, or the incredible migratory kūaka/godwits.

Near the coast, you'll see the exposed volcanic lava flow which once spewed from nearby Māngere Mountain about 18,000 years ago. The molten lava river flowed at speeds of up to 30 kilometres an hour and roasted everything in its way, with temperatures of more than 1100 degrees Celsius.

But sometimes the molten lava in the centre of the flow drained

INFORMATION

GRADE: Easy

ACCESSIBILITY: Flat grass and dirt paths. Occasional boggy patches.

TIME: 45 min (about 2 km) return.

LOCATION: Trail starts beside the Ambury Regional Park car park (p148).

DOGS: No dogs allowed.

TITIWAI | GLOW-WORMS

Glow-worms are not real worms. They are the larvae/maggots of a fungus gnat fly which looks similar to a mosquito.

They love damp spots with still and humid air where they can dangle their sticky threads to attract and snare flying insects. They are often found on the roof of a cave or on overhanging damp forest banks.

Interestingly, the mature fly is not attracted to the light, so cannot be caught.

Titiwai refers to lights reflected in water.

SOUTH AUCKLAND

away to leave tubes or caves. There are a few of these small caves that kids can explore along the way – as long as they are not squeamish about cave wētā or glow-worms!

This area was once clad in a dense forest of taraire, pūriri and pōhutukawa trees which were home to thousands of birds. It was cleared by early Māori settlers to plant food crops. A restoration project is underway at the native herb field and saltmarsh, which are home to some unique and rare plants.

ACCESSIBILITY

If you keep to the grass and hop across the small boggy patches in winter, you'll make it out of this adventure with clean shoes. But some mud-sploshing near the coastline adds to the fun. The walk is not suitable for bikes, wheelchairs or buggies.

Saline herb field

153

SOUTH AUCKLAND

MĀNGERE
WATERCARE COASTAL WALKWAY

After visiting the cute animals at Ambury Regional Park (p148), jump on your bike for this family-friendly adventure which takes in the highlights of the Ōtuataua Stonefields (p156), nearby bird hides and Māngere Lagoon (p151).

INFORMATION

GRADE: Medium

TIME: 1–2 hours return.

DISTANCE: 7 km one-way or as short as you'd like.

LOCATION: The main starting point is from Ambury Regional Park car park (p148).

FACILITIES: Toilet available at the start and another towards the end.

DOGS: No dogs allowed.

If the kids are keen to graduate to a longer trail ride, this cycling and walking trail is perfect. If little legs tire along the way, this out-and-back route can easily be shortened.

Follow the signs south through a couple of farm gates from the central car park at Ambury to the start of the trail. About 1 kilometre along the well-graded gravel path, you can turn right and follow the bird hide signs. This route is more scenic than continuing straight ahead – although both options do connect up further along.

At the hide, kids will be able to use the bird identification guides and peer through the wooden windows to see if they can spy some of the country's native birds. This area is a nesting ground for the endangered tūturiwhatu/New Zealand dotterel that builds its nests above the high-tide mark on the beach – which makes them especially vulnerable to dogs and predators.

MATUKU MOANA
REEF HERON

These stealthy native birds stalk around rocky shorelines and estuary mudflats on the hunt for small critters including crustaceans, worms and small fish.

The bird is nationally endangered, and its population of only 300 to 500 is mainly located in the northern areas of the North Island.

It looks similar to the matuku moana/white-faced heron but is dark grey, and less commonly spotted. It is very wary and will fly away if approached too closely.

SOUTH AUCKLAND

The wide track is relatively flat as you hug the coastline towards the water treatment plant, and further afield to the Ōtuataua Stonefields.

You'll pedal past nearly 300,000 native trees planted by Watercare and local community groups, which are providing food and shelter to native birds and other migratory birds that arrive here to escape the cold northern winter.

The path ends shortly after the information panels beside the shoreline at Ōtuataua Stonefields. From here, you can continue down to the shell beach for an explore, before returning the way you came. Add on the Māngere Lagoon as a little diversion on the way back to the farm.

155

SOUTH AUCKLAND

IHUMĀTAO | MĀNGERE
ŌTUATAUA STONEFIELDS HISTORIC RESERVE

This rugged site is an internationally significant heritage landscape that offers an insight into some of the earliest Polynesian settlement of New Zealand. Only a handful of stonefield remnants remain in Auckland, so this unique spot holds important horticultural lessons.

The Auckland isthmus once had 8,000 hectares of volcanic stonefields; today, just 160 hectares remain. Ōtuataua Stonefields is a sprawling site with a fascinating history of cultivating kūmara, yams and taro. The warm volcanic stone extended the area's growing seasons. Various settlement dates at Ōtuataua likely occurred but ongoing settlement by Polynesians possibly began 750 years ago. Even as recently as two centuries ago, the stonefields were under cultivation. However, following the 1800s Musket Wars, and the encroachment of urban sprawl, just a small fraction remains.

Near the reserve's entrance, a map shows three self-guided walks which focus on geology, botany and history with different-coloured markers to follow. Or, explore the sprawling site free-range. You can still see remnants of the Polynesian house sites and various cultivation areas, midden sites containing shell and stone (these areas were essentially dumping grounds for domestic waste), garden walls, plots, mound gardens and terraces.

Ōtuataua Stonefields became a historic reserve in 2001, and Auckland Council manages the reserve as a farm park. Manukau City Council initially purchased the 100-hectare site with assistance from the NZ Lotteries Commission, the then Auckland Regional Council and the Department of Conservation.

TOILETS
There are no toilets on site. The nearest toilets are located at Oruarangi, about one kilometre north of the main entrance gate.

AVOCADO ORCHARD
Visit the orchard and grab a few ripe fruit to take home. A maximum of five avocados per person is allowed. Avocados generally ripen from November through to March.

KIWI ADVENTURES

NEW ZEALAND'S TRAIL
TE ARAROA

Te Araroa is the ultimate New Zealand tramping experience. This 3,000-kilometre walking track from Cape Reinga to Bluff connects settlements, townships and cities. It is billed as a corridor that encourages social and economic transactions en route – from marae stays to handwritten signs by locals offering accommodation to hikers.

Te Araroa's boundaries are the natural boundaries of New Zealand itself. It starts from and is brought to a natural halt by the sea.

New Zealand's volcanoes, ranges, mountains, rivers, lakes and valleys are on show. Te Araroa's variety is underpinned by the mightiest geology of all – tectonic plate movement. When walking New Zealand, you are also walking the Pacific Plate boundary and, at times, the Ring of Fire.

HISTORY

1975: The New Zealand Walkways Commission is formed. One of its goals was the creation of a scenic trail the length of New Zealand.

1983–1984: Taranaki man Rex Hendry did a wilderness walk that explored a possible route for a long New Zealand trail.

1994: Te Araroa Trust is formed after a newspaper article by Geoff Chapple was published, advocating for a trail the length of New Zealand.

1997: Te Araroa Trust maps a North Island route.

1998: Geoff Chapple walks the northern route to prove its viability.

2002: Geoff Chapple walks the southern route to prove its viability.

2011: Te Araroa officially opened by Governor-General Sir Jerry Mateparae.

FIND OUT MORE
teararoa.org.nz

IMPORTANT

The reserve is wāhi tapu/a sacred place. Visitors cannot consume food here, although water bottles are welcome.

An excellent trail map can be downloaded from the Auckland Council website.

INFORMATION

GRADE: Medium

ACCESSIBILITY: Various dirt and grass paths. At times uneven with steps.

TIME: 1 hour to 1 hour and 30 min for a free-range explore.

LOCATION: Plenty of parking at the end of Ihumātao Quarry Road, Ihumātao, Māngere.

DOGS: On leads.

SOUTH AUCKLAND

TOYOTA KIWI GUARDIANS
AUCKLAND BOTANIC GARDENS

This family-friendly park in South Auckland has loads of unique themed areas to explore. Don't miss the educational Potter Children's Garden and the amazing palm-lined Puhinui Stream Forest Trail. There are loads of places to enjoy a picnic, and the family pooch is welcome too!

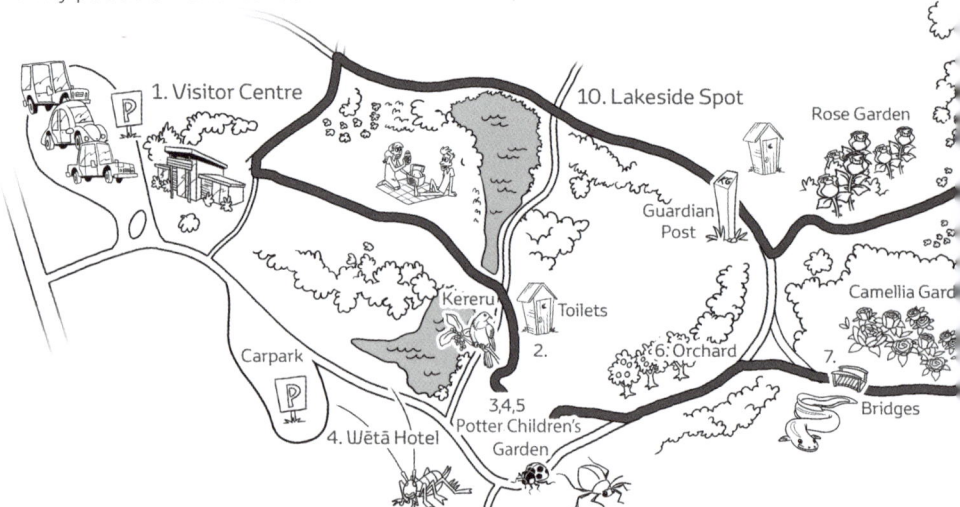

This adventure is part of the Toyota Kiwi Guardians programme. Before you visit, download an activity sheet from kiwiguardians.co.nz or use the one in this book. Claim a medal when you find the unique code written on the Kiwi Guardian Post.

1. HUAKAIWAKA VISITOR CENTRE: Check out the amazing exhibits and ask the staff if they have any activities for you to do.

2. CHILDREN'S GARDEN TOILETS: These toilets are a bit different. Do you know why they're good for the gardens?

3. KERERŪ AND PŪRIRI: Keri the kererū is hiding somewhere. Can you find where he is and why he likes the pūriri tree?

4. WĒTĀ SPOTTING: Can you see the wētā chilling in the hotel? Create your own custom-made wētā hotel at home to earn a Kiwi Guardian Action Medal.

5. GRUBS UP: Jump into the wonderful world of bugs. How many can you see? Make a list!

6. ORCHARD: Juicy fruit dangles from the trees in autumn. How many different types of fruit trees can you see?

7. BRIDGES: Can you see the tuna/eels slithering through the stream? What else can you see living down there? You may even see some kōura/freshwater crayfish.

8. BIRDLIFE: Stop and listen for two minutes. Can you find the loudest bird in the bush?

9. NATIVE FOREST: Look at all the different trees and plants. How many different shapes can you see?

10. LAKESIDE SPOT: Great work! Now sit down, take a break and play 'I spy'.

Image and content courtesy of Toyota Kiwi Guardians.

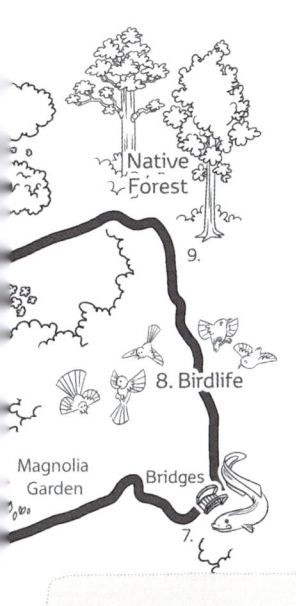

SOUTH AUCKLAND

THE GARDENS
PUHINUI STREAM FOREST TRAIL

This adventure begins at the far end of the Auckland Botanic Gardens and feels like a tropical oasis. Stroll under the palm trees, listen out for the native birds, then loop back to the start past a scenic waterfall.

Take your time heading up the Lookout Walk and peek through the trees to the suburbs surrounding the Gardens. Smaller kids may ask for a piggy-back for this steady climb. Follow the trail onto the Puhinui Stream Forest Trail and back to the Waterfall Walk. This walk takes in all the highlights and is an outing that meanders through a variety of different forest types: from kauri, pūriri, tōtara to nīkau. The forest is an excellent example of a lowland broadleaf conifer forest. Combined with the nearby Tōtara Park, the area has a total of 155 native plant species – so bring along your native plant guidebook and get identifying! Peek in the wētā motels attached to the trees to see if any of these ancient critters are chilling out at home.

INFORMATION

GRADE: Easy

ACCESSIBILITY: Suitable for buggies and wheelchairs except after the bridge to 8 and 9 (birdlife and native forest).

TIME: Allow 1 hour (2 km) to complete the loop.

LOCATION: Park at the main car park, off SH1 Southern Motorway on Hill Road, The Gardens.

DOGS: On leads.

INFORMATION

GRADE: Easy/Medium

ACCESSIBILITY: Well-graded dirt paths (some steep) and steps.

TIME: 1 hour for a casual explore.

LOCATION: Park at Auckland Botanic Gardens, Hill Road, The Gardens.

DOGS: On leads.

SOUTH AUCKLAND

TŌTARA PARK
TŌTARA PARK MTB TRACK

This sprawling 216-hectare park is home to one of the best family-friendly mountain bike parks in the city.

More than 14 kilometres of trail wind through rolling farmland with grazing cattle, through stands of regenerating native bush and across a handful of shallow streams.

There's plenty of visibility throughout most of the farm park, which is great for biking as a family. A couple of gnarly sections will suit more advanced intermediate riders, but in general the intermediate graded trails will suit confident riders of all ages. There is one advanced trail, Mawhitiwhiti, which has some challenging jumps.

From the upper car park, the trail dives straight down the ridge on Fatmans Revenge to The Hub. This central clearing has tables to relax at and is the ideal place to map out your adventure on the quality trails built by volunteers of the Tōtara Park Mountain Bike Club since 2013.

From The Hub, there are plenty of fun flowy trails departing in all directions, including the intermediate 2.7-kilometre Pony Express trail. Newbies can zip along the easy Beginners Loop (400 metres long) which starts from the clearing too. It has a few corners, some ups and downs but nothing too serious, and is ideal for learning the ropes on mountain bikes.

There's also a small pump track near The Hub for a quick tear around and to burn off any remaining energy.

All the trails are well signposted, and bikers have the right of way. Just remember to leave enough in the tank to get the kids back up the hill to the car park.

HOW TO GET THERE

Take the Manukau exit off SH1 onto Redoubt Road. The park is about 1.5 kilometres further along on the right. Allow about 20 minutes from downtown Auckland.

Image © Daniel Newman

TŌTARA PARK MOUNTAIN BIKE CLUB

Get among the action by joining the Tōtara Park Mountain Bike Club.

The Club's keen volunteers are passionate about building one of the best mountain bike parks in Auckland and host plenty of club days for all ages.

Find out more about joining or lending a hand on the tracks at their website.

FIND OUT MORE
tpmtbc.org.nz

KIWI ADVENTURES

ON TWO WHEELS
GREAT RIDES APP

No cartographer (a person who draws or produces maps) likes getting lost on a bike trail, so Gary Patterson created an app to find his way.

'I developed the app because I love exploring but less so feeling lost! After riding a southern trail a few years ago and getting disorientated, I thought there must be an app out there to help me with each cycle trail. There was none. Given my career as a cartographer, mountain-bike-trail designer and builder, coupled with a personal love of the NZ Cycle Trail, I decided to make a free app.

FIND OUT MORE
greatridesapp.com

This led to a fascinating journey riding our country's greatest trails and recording features to create this personal trail guide. I designed the app to help visitors pick, plan and plot their way around cycle trails of the region. It's easy to get as it is free from the App or Play stores; you can review the trails that interest you and download the trail. Once you do this, it works offline for when you go out and play.'

GREAT HIKES APP

The app now has a buddy called the Great Hikes App for the Department of Conservation's Great Walks. It is free to download and is just as handy as the cycling app: greathikesapp.com

INFORMATION

WHAT FACILITIES ARE IN THE PARK? A portaloo on the Bridal Veil trail. Toilets near the Wairere Road entrance. Tables at The Hub.

WHAT GRADES ARE THE TRAIL? A mix of Grade 2 (Easy) and Grade 3 (Intermediate).

WHEN IS THE PARK OPEN? The trails are accessible 24 hours but check the signs for the car park closure times.

HOW MUCH DOES IT COST TO RIDE IN THE PARK? No charge. A donation to Tōtara Park Mountain Bike Club is always appreciated.

ARE E-BIKES ALLOWED ON THE TRAIL? Pedal-assist e-bikes are welcome.

ARE DOGS ALLOWED ON THE TRAIL? Yes, but they need to be kept under control for everyone's safety.

IMPORTANT: There's minimal shade here – so remember to slip, slop, slap and wrap. Bring plenty of water and snacks for the kids.

GREAT RIDES APP
NZ'S ONLY MOBILE APP FOR ALL THE GREAT RIDES

Pick • any of the 23 NZ Great Rides + bonus trails
Plan • using 2,000+ pages of photos/maps/guides
Plot • with accurate offline tracking & content

FREE DOWNLOAD

Download on the App Store | GET IT ON Google Play

www.greatridesapp.com

161

NATURE DISCOVERY

CAN YOU SPY ANY OF THESE
AMAZING NATIVE CRITTERS?

There are thousands of different insect species in New Zealand, and because of our isolation, more than 90 per cent are not found anywhere else in the world.

HUHU GRUB

NGĀOKEOKE | PERIPATUS/VELVET WORM

KAPOKAPOWAI BUSH GIANT DRAGONFLY

KIHIKIHI-WAWĀ CHORUS CICADA

WĒTĀ

PŪRIRI MOTH

KAHUKURA RED ADMIRAL BUTTERFLY

Te Papa Atawhai | Department of Conservation
Te Taura Whiri i te Reo Māori | Māori Language Commission
Te Tāhuhu o te Mātauranga | Ministry of Education

Kia Kaha te Reo Taiao

Language of the Environment
Give it a Go!

WHAKAHUATANGA | PRONUNCIATION

Oropuare | Vowels

There are five vowel sounds in Māori. They can be pronounced 'short' or 'long'. The long vowel is marked with a macron.

a is close or similar to f**a**ther

e is close or similar to dr**e**ss

i is close or similar to s**ee**

o is close or similar to th**o**ught

u is close or similar to g**oo**se

a e i o u
ā ē ī ō ū

When the vowel is long, with a macron above it, say the vowel for twice as long.

Ororua | Two Vowels and Diphthongs

When two different vowels are together they either retain their basic sounds and are pronounced one after the other or they 'glide' from one vowel to the other vowel to make a different sound we call a diphthong. Examples of common diphthongs are ai, ae, au, ou, oe, ao.

ai oe
ae au
ou ao

Orokati | Consonants

There are 10 consonants, they are:

h k m n ng
p r t w wh

ng as in si**ng**er

wh as in **f**ilm

r is usually not rolled. The r sound is created when the tip of the tongue briefly touches the top of the mouth behind the teeth.

Me haere tāua ki te kaukau!
Let's go for a swim!

He makariri te wai?
Is the water cold?

Hei aha te kirihou, kei te whakaiti au i te nui o aku para
No plastic thanks, I am trying to cut down on waste

Ko Te Ika-a-Māui tērā, ko Te Waipounamu, ko Rakiura rānei?
Is that the North Island, the South Island, or Stewart Island?

Kia haumaru, kia kitea
Be safe, be seen

Haria ko ngā maharatanga anake, waiho ko ngā tapuae anake
Take nothing but memories, leave nothing but footprints

- **Tangaroa** God of Sea
- **Hinemoana** Female Guardian of the Sea
- **tai** tide
- **ngā ngaru** waves
- **rimurimu** seaweed
- **tohorā** southern right whale
- **paikea** humpback whale
- **parāoa** sperm whale
- **takutai one** sandy beach
- **ākau** rocky beach
- **tātahi** to the beach or on the beach
- **tahatai** beach
- **papawai, hāroto** rock pools
- **kirikiri** sand
- **kōhatu, toka** rock
- **kōura** crayfish
- **ika, ngohi** fish
- **wai ora, wai māori** healthy water

Mai i ngā maunga ki te moana
Mountains to the sea

He aha ka kitea i te wai?
What can you see in the water?

- **taniwha** — guardian protector
- **kapowai** — dragonfly
- **kōtuku** — white heron
- **piharau, kanakana** — lamprey
- **tuna** — eel
- **īnanga** — whitebait
- **whio** — blue duck
- **kōkopu** — giant bully
- **mātāwainuku** — underground aquifer
- **korio, tāheke** — rapids
- **kēwai, kōura wai māori** — freshwater crayfish
- **hīrere, tāheke** — waterfall
- **puna kaukau** — swimming hole
- **awa** — river, stream
- **moana, roto** — lake
- **wai māori** — fresh water
- **kōhatu awa** — river stone
- **repo** — wetlands

Me tūpato ki te rere o te wai
Be careful of the current

Me kaukau tāua ki te awa
Let's meet at the river for a swim

Kaua e taraiwa i runga i te kūkūpango
Don't drive on the riverbed

Kaua e whakakino i te wai
Don't pollute the water

Tiakina a Papatūānuku

Protect the Earth Mother

ongaonga stinging nettle

māra kai cultivation and vegetable garden

kōpurawhetū – werewere kōkako native fungi – blue mushroom

rongoā medicine

āniwaniwa, uenuku rainbow

Me hīkoi haere tāua i te puihi ā ngā rā whakatā?
Shall we go for a bushwalk this weekend?

Me mahara ki te whakapaipai i ō hū
Remember to clean your shoes

pūtu hīkoi tramping boots

whenua land

ngahere forest

ara track

nīkau palm tree

pikopiko edible fern shoots

kōtaratara Māori holly

patupaiarehe fairy people

tawhai beech tree

He aha te rākau hei whakatō mā tāua?
What tree shall we plant?

Me mātua whai i te ara
Stay on the track

ponga silver fern

kōtukutuku fuchsia

puihi bush

rau leaf

rautini Chatham Island Christmas tree

tātarāmoa bush lawyer vine

pōānanga native clematis

Aue! Whakarongo ki te kōkī hāpara

Wow! Listen to the dawn chorus

Waimarie katoa tātou ki te kite i te tini o ngā kererū i konei
We are so lucky to see so many kererū here

I kite au i te kōtuku i te rangi nei
I saw a kōtuku today

He pūkeko tērā, he takahē rānei?
Is that a pūkeko or a takahē?

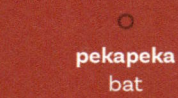

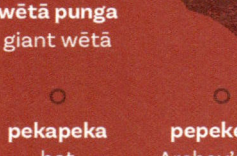

mohua	yellowhead
pīwakawaka / pīwaiwaka	fantail
tīrairaka	fantail
tīeke	saddleback
manu	bird
pīpīwharauroa	shining cuckoo
kāhu	hawk
ruru	morepork
pepeke	insect
ngārara	insect
tuatara	reptile
mokomoko	lizard
wētā punga	giant wētā
pekapeka	bat
pepeketua	Archey's frog
pepetuna	pūriri moth
ngata	giant snail
ngaro huruhuru	native bee